On *Measure for Measure*

Detail of tapestry: *The Redemption of Man,* from Burgos Cathedral, discussed in note 36. Flemish, Brussels. 16th C., ca. 1500. Probably woven in the workshops of Pieter Van Aelst. The Metropolitan Museum of Art, Fletcher Fund, 1938. (38.29)

On *Measure for Measure*

An Essay in Criticism of Shakespeare's Drama

Lawrence J. Ross

DELAWARE

Newark: University of Delaware Press
London: Associated University Presses

Associated University Presses
440 Forsgate Drive
Cranbury, NJ 08512

Associated University Presses
16 Barter Street
London WC1A 2AH, England

Associated University Presses
P.O. Box 338, Port Credit
Mississauga, Ontario
Canada L5G 4L8

The paper used in this publication meets the requirements
of the American National Standard for Permanence of Paper
for Printed Library Materials Z39.48–1984.

Library of Congress Cataloging-in-Publication Data

Ross, Lawrence J., 1926–1996
    On Measure for measure : an essay in criticism of Shakespeare's
drama / Lawrence J. Ross.
        p. cm.
    Includes bibliographical references (p.   ) and index.
    ISBN 0-87413-593-1 (alk. paper)
    1. Shakespeare, William, 1564–1616.   Measure for measure.
I. Title.
PR2824.R67   1997
822.3'3—dc21   96-48852
                                                                    CIP

PRINTED IN THE UNITED STATES OF AMERICA

To the memory of
Gerald Eades Bentley

Contents

Publisher's Note

REGRETFULLY, this book is being published posthumously. On 23 January 1996, just days before receiving the copyedited manuscript, Dr. Lawrence J. Ross died of a heart attack. Dr. Ross was therefore unable to review the copyedited manuscript, the galleys, or the page proofs, and thus bears no responsibility for any errors that may have made their way into the published text. The only substantive aspects of this book over which Dr. Ross did not have complete authorial control are a few copyediting changes, which were meticulously made by his daughter, Jenny E. Ross, with the aim of carefully preserving Dr. Ross's intended meaning. Ms. Ross was assisted in this task by Dr. Joseph R. Roach and Ms. Anne T. Makeever. In addition, the index for the book was prepared by a professional indexer.

Preface

Of the plays presented as Shakespeare's comedies in the First Folio, *Measure for Measure* probably has been the most discussed in this century. It certainly has been the one play that has produced the most multiplicitous, fundamental, and unresolved critical disagreement. That those who praise it no more agree than those who deplore it does not begin to tell the story. No other Shakespearean play has evinced such wildly varying and contradictory responses. Such pronounced incoherence in the criticism of a work of Shakespeare's maturity, a play selected for performance at court, must strike us as decidedly odd. Surely it sorts ill with the play's position in the dramatist's career. *Measure for Measure* was composed by Shakespeare at the height of his powers. It was the finale of the three experimental plays composed by him between *Hamlet* and *Othello*. The just-previous instance of ending his work of a particular kind produced the past-masterly *Twelfth Night*. And *Measure for Measure* is singular; there really is nothing quite like it in the entire surviving corpus of "Elizabethan" drama. I think the conclusion we must draw is the same one urged by the extremely contradictory nature of the criticism and by its inability to find any whole in which the admired parts of the play can fit, to agree about the nature of principal characters, or to reach anything but confused stalemate about the play's self-consciously elaborate ending. We must entertain as likelihood that what may be wanting is not the play, but rather our ways of apprehending and construing it.

Shakespeare has often, and justly, been said to be a touchstone of criticism. Of all the plays, *Measure for Measure* may be the best one to test the adequacy of any way proposed for doing the business of criticism with Shakespearean drama—including the eclectic historical sort of dramatic criticism attempted here. The present study, in offering a new interpretation of the play that confronts and claims to deal with the problems it poses, constitutes such a test of the critical conceptions and practices that produced it.

9

Whether it passes that test or not is for the reader to say. But to the extent it does pass, then its assumptions and methods have a more general importance for Shakespeare studies. My title, thus, is twofold in intent. The book is about Shakespeare's *Measure for Measure*. But "measure for measure" I take to be an ideal of criticism and what that may mean for criticism of Shakespearean drama is simultaneously what the book is about too.

The first assumption is that the work is neither apprehensible nor comprehensible except in terms of what it primarily is. It is a play, and that must be—for earlier it has not been—our continuous and fundamental consideration. The play assumes the physicality in time and space of stage performance before an audience. That makes *Measure for Measure* essentially different from *The Faerie Queene,* and makes the problem of addressing ourselves to them different too. The theater, as the play's proper environment, certainly is one place we must study it, even if that must be a theater very different from the sort for which the play was created. But any performance can only present a production's representation of the play. No performance, however illuminating of the play, *is* the play anymore, indeed, than the text is. Most Shakespeare criticism is literary, which can take us some distance as the plays presuppose a deeply language-dependent theatrical transaction. But we must always be dealing with speech and poetry in the service of drama; and the elements required for the theatrical realization of that drama are parts of the "poem." Ironically, it is exactly because of the import of the text *in the theater* that we have so substantial a literary object called Shakespeare to talk about. There would be no play without the text, but the text is not the play.

Still, the received text is our only primary evidence of, and means through which we can get to, the Shakespeare play that we should be trying critically to experience. Apart from changes suffered in transmission (and editorial alteration), a good text such as that of *Measure for Measure* represents what the professional theater and book trade both regarded as "the book of the play," that is, the basis for the regulation of its performance. What we have in the text is the extant provision for representing Shakespeare's play in performance in accord with the theatrical conditions and conventions then prevailing. To be sure, we must acquire sufficient knowledge to respond appropriately to the book-of-the-play's notation, and there can be no evading construal in our reading to have a play to criticize. However, though all reading necessarily is construction, it does not follow that all constructions are readings. Among his provisions for performance, Shakespeare, the complete professional of the theater, took care to include improvisational space for the players' art in what must be a complexly collaborative enterprise. But examination shows that, governing that freedom, boundary conditions, obligations to the play, and functions in behalf of it are carefully indicated. Shakespeare made the play, and we are not at liberty to devise it as we will or as any argument of ours may require. Our endeavor cannot be to lead the very witness whose purpose was to regulate the play's realization. Anything we say of the play must be shown to have warrant based in what Shakespeare has "set down" (*Hamlet* III.ii.39) to be performed.

Such a reading must be historically founded in very wide-ranging precritical studies so we can acquire what Ben Jonson called the needed "wits to read" Shakespeare's "book"—if his play is to live in our experience. We cannot pretend to be reading Shakespeare unless we read his plays as plays, and in the "language"—in the widest requisite sense of that word—in which he wrote. Some things implied here merit immediate notice. We need all the knowledge we can get about what used to be called intellectual and other "backgrounds," so we can deploy it where and as Shakespeare demonstrably uses them—in the play as it is "set down" to unfold on the stage. Shakespeare is extraordinarily dependent in this play on a rich variety of intellectual, literary, and dramatic traditions and conventions, received ideas and contemporary argument and reference. Much of this has been usefully if not conclusively explored, though some ideas quite crucial to the play have been missed that were demonstrably part of the stock of stuff the audience originally brought to the theater for the dramatist to exploit. *Measure for Measure* has been a notable locus for debate about how we are to deal with Shakespeare's use of received thought about the truly remarkable range of subjects and issues his play entertains. Our learning in this regard as in others must be to identify what Shakespeare has used and above all how and to what end he has dramatically used it. A related point about our reading—and I think a profound and far-reaching one—is that Shakespearean drama suffuses its content in the medium of the theater, in particular of a theater where the playwright has great control over what there is for an audience to attend to and how it will be placed to attend to it. Indeed, the dramatist's manipulation of the audience, defining its participation in, and finally its relation to, the play must be a major critical concern if the play is to be read on its own terms, that is, as a play and in the "language" in which he created; for the audience constitutes an essential part of the consort for which the dramatist composes.

The last point needing emphasis from the outset is that we must continually be concerned with the dramaturgy. The playwright's use of conventions and methods of representation in drama and staging, his treatment of the relation of agent, action, and scene, his management of exposition, preparation, focus, suspense, and surprise, his symmetric, iterative, and analogical designs—all these are essential. But our indispensable study must be the dramaturgical structure. For in the structure are to be found the clearest ideas about what the play is doing and saying, and it must figure in everything we think and feel about the play. Here is a point that needs immediate illustration because of the very inattention to it that has prevailed. Anyone who sees the play in performance (if it is not cut or rearranged) will come to Isabella and Angelo's first interview directly following experience of the judicial hearing about Pompey the parcel-bawd's attempt to enlist Elbow's wife. We hear nothing about that in criticism of the famous scene that follows. Again, Isabella and Claudio's "scene" together in the prison is an obligatory one in criticism of the play. But these characters are not alone onstage and most important their dialogue is, dramaturgically, not a *scene* at all but rather an example of the basic dramaturgical units, running from one entrance or exit to the next, out of which scenes are built. In the scene of which their grouping is a part, neither character is the principal one. The point is of prime importance because it is in the very midst of *that* scene that an irredeemable "split" in the play supposedly occurs.

Some comment might usefully be made here about the extraordinary difficulty of representing a play discursively so that it can be critically entertained for what it is, and what it is saying through what it is. The play that we are trying to grasp and represent in discourse from the evidence of the provisions for its representation in performance is an experienced thing that happens in time. What the whole is seen to be must depend on the dramatic process by which it *becomes*. We thus have to try to be very clear about temporal perspective in connection with any attempt at generalization, in views of the completed whole, and in reference to any part of the play. Such considerations speak to scruple and techniques in my own critical practice following. Whatever our interest in an overall aspect of a play, any particular should be cited with respect to the force it has by position in the experienced unfolding of the action. I have also used iterative techniques whereby we are returned to part of the play already considered. I believe these to be necessary because the bias of concern in critical discourse at any moment is fairly sure to do less than justice to the intrinsically multifaceted character of any part. One does not want to be tedious in an attempt bound to fall short no matter what one's contrivance. Yet critical discourse must somehow more seriously contend with what certainly is not the least of the basic difficulties in representing Shakespeare. We have Shakespearean scope and capaciousness to cope with; on the other hand, his drama is a highly condensed art characteristically presenting at every point a dense simultaneity of expression.

I would argue that what is being conducted in this book, with whatever insufficiency, is at root cognitive inquiry. Though my limitations cannot let me hope I have entirely succeeded, I have tried to be objective—with what achievement in view it is important to say. In her introduction to a fine volume of essays, Helen Vendler writes of the need of repeated critical efforts until a poem is "finally known." For my own part, I do not think there can be such a thing as "last word" criticism, any more than there can be ultimate utterance about the nature of physical reality. That position is not taken because I am writing on a challenging play— I think perhaps Shakespeare's most sophisticated one—that altered the possibilities of drama, although I am; it is held in principle. But I certainly do believe in the possibility of "first word" criticism, or perhaps better said, *sine qua non* criticism—that without which we cannot hope to proceed with approximate truth to the object. That is what is attempted here.

Our unique text of *Measure for Measure* is preserved in the First Folio (sig. F^r–[G6]^v). References, where required, are by Through Line Number in the Norton facsimile of the Folio prepared by Charlton Hinman. But for convenience I have cited the play throughout from the 1965 Arden edition by J. W. Lever. Differences from this edition are indicated, and textual problems (actual or supposed) of major critical consequence are treated in the course of my argument and attendant notes. Shakespeare's other plays are cited from *The Riverside Shakespeare* (1974).

Attempting such a work as this cannot but heighten the writer's awareness of profound indebtedness to the vast community of learning over time on which it necessarily depends. My text and notes cannot adequately specify this. Indeed, I do not name all of the Shakespeare studies, even those comprising the extensive literature on this play, from which I have learned so much, not least from those that have developed my understanding through difference with them.

I am grateful to Joseph R. Roach for invaluable detailed criticism of an earlier version of this study and for his deep appreciation of my purpose. John Velz's timely reading called my attention to several major points needing further clarification. Jay Halio helpfully suggested that I consider a few very recent arguments bearing on the subject published since my work was first submitted. Others, who read and commented on earlier drafts, not only sustained me in the project but allowed me to test the work on different audiences, helped me to refine the argument, and to make it more readable. I take pleasure in thanking Judiah Higgins, Michaela Giesenkirchen, Diane Roberts, and my extraordinarily reliable and editorially acute computer typist, Anne T. Makeever.

On *Measure for Measure*

On *Measure for Measure*

THE unique fascination that *Measure for Measure* has held for this century, which has given the play a prominence never earlier enjoyed in its vexed critical history, has been expressed in a large mass of writings remarkably various, contradictory, and contortionate. As Ernest Schanzer observes, no other of Shakespeare's plays has called forth "such violent, eccentric, and mutually opposed responses."[1] This critical literature, by what it has opened up in attempts to deal with the play, arguably has expanded rather than contracted the area of disagreement about it, just as the plethora of formulations of the play's substance has confirmed rather than removed our sense of its problematic character. Nor is this situation changed by assuming that the more extreme views cancel out each other. *Measure for Measure* cannot be both an allegory of the Atonement (Battenhouse) and the play in which "the lowest depths of Jacobean cynicism are touched" (Ellis-Fermor)[2], and it is most unlikely to be either. But rejecting these particular views does not eliminate the obligation to cope with the play's deep interest in both Christian thought and ironic perspective.

This conflicted body of criticism—by its very size and multiplicity, its compelling immediacy, and the intensity of its preoccupations—can be an obstacle to our coming at the play with hope of fresh apprehension. Like a volcanic mountain rapidly risen out of the troubled earth, it threatens to occupy our horizon, blocking the view of what we might hope to see. There is reason to be concerned lest its conceptions, orderings, and emphases displace what might be the play's. If the Folio text in which it survives and all derivative texts were suddenly to vanish, what has been written about the play might serve to recover much of its opening, two major scenes in which its main character does not appear, and a highly dramatic part of another in which, by and large, he would not be remembered as appearing. The striking long finale would be recalled less dependably, blurred by clouded crosswinds of debate and biased memory. (It is astonishing how many writers refer to the "marriage" or "betrothal" of the Duke and Isabella or, more sourly, to her declining "coyly into the ex-Friar's bosom" [Rossiter].)[3] Several much-discussed speeches elsewhere could be reclaimed via different interpretations, as could a number of other vivid moments as well, but many of these would be so reclaimed with no sure sense of their connectedness in the whole. For the principal *dramatis persona,* who speaks almost a third of the play's lines, we would be left with a few mutually exclusive views and the detective's identification kit critics have tried on him. On the other hand, the very sharpness of the biases in views of the heroine might render her more clearly, as in a double exposure. As for the play's third longest role, it surely would be misidentified as belonging to the strongly delineated corrupted deputy, who is not onstage for the whole of the middle of the play (between II.iv and IV.iv).

The criticism would lead us to surmise, as it does where preoccupation with character study permits, that this play deals with a powerful nexus of issues about matters radical to our humanity. These issues—spiritual and religious, political, social, moral, psychological, and physical—are such as are bound to engage, even disturb us, sufficiently indeed to bring our prejudices into play, as questions of authority, government, religion, justice, liberty, death, vice, and sexuality tend to do. In developing these issues, *Measure for Measure* is, to a degree unusual for Shakespeare, frontally insistent upon its consideration of ideas. That fact inevitably has led students, in their frustration and puzzlement at the play, to seek for keys to solutions outside it, in Elizabethan law, in Scripture and Christian doctrine, in the "givings forth" of King James, and elsewhere.

The play has thus become the hottest battleground for the continuing argument over the use of such reference in Shakespearean criticism. Certainly this is a play that raises in acute form the question of how we are to deal critically with Shakespeare's use of received ideas and conventions of thought. Students of the various backgrounds have taught us much we need to know to read the play well, but whether they have read it well is a very different matter. The play appears to tempt premature closure and partiality of response. It is perfect bait to catch us in the frailty of pursuing a wished consistency and treating the text accordingly. Reference to systems of thought particularly involve risks of assimilating the play to the system. In these kinds of studies one finds much imposition of matter on the play, substitutions of background for its own matter, and biased selection from the play and the background. But in Shakespeare's time as now, responses to the issues raised were not univocal, nor could Shakespeare expect them to be. The hunger for straightforward—not to say simplistic—answers to inherently doubtful questions is critically self-thwarting. The play's habitude, though often exercised covertly, is in debate; its text is everywhere sensitive to contradiction. This Shakespeare is the same dramatist who had so calculatingly exploited in *Hamlet* the controversy about ghosts to enforce audience awareness of the dubiety of its circumstance. That the most fundamental verities assumed by his age were surrounded by controversy or fraught with contradiction at the level of human experience, he took pains to remind the audience of this play, early in its second scene where the world to be governed is first exhibited:

1 Gent.   . . . There's not a soldier of us all that, in the thanksgiving before meat, do relish the petition well that prays for peace.

2 Gent.   . . . I never heard any soldier dislike it.

Lucio.   I believe thee; for I think thou never wast where grace was said.

2 Gent.   No? A dozen times at least.

1 Gent.   What, in metre?

Lucio.   In any proportion, or in any language.

1 Gent.   I think, or in any religion.

Lucio.   Ay, why not? Grace is grace, despite of all controversy; as for example, thou thyself art a wicked villain, despite of all grace.

1 Gent.   Well, there went but a pair of shears between us.

(I.ii.14–27)

The other principal point that could be surmised from its criticism is that the play is quite as problematic in form as in content. To many the structure seems radically flawed: the play split down the middle at the Duke's intervention with a shift in style, treatment of the matter, and even mode of representation. The low comic matter, sometimes found objectionable, not seldom elbowed out of view, has failed to appear integral to the design. And whether, or how, the conclusion can be supposed to fit what precedes is intensely debated. These considerations are inseparable from the radical uncertainty about the play's genre. The Folio editors placed it among the comedies, of course. Many, however, have vehemently regarded the play as a tragedy betrayed. F. R. Leavis never did put down "the old prepotent tradition" whose doubts and dissatisfactions have "placed *Measure for Measure* . . . among the unconscionable compromises of the artist with the botcher, the tragic poet with the slick provider of bespoke comedy."[4]

In view of the seriousness of the issues and the real evil behind Angelo's threat in the action, some would call the play a tragicomedy. But the passages cited in justification from Guarini's theorizing about tragicomedy[5] bear no clear and useful, let alone definitive, relation to this play, and the Italian's practice is utterly unlike whatever Shakespeare here attempted. Nor is *Measure for Measure* similar either to Marston's contemporary *The Malcontent,* advertized as "tragaecomedy" on its title page, or to the later kinds of tragicomedy Beaumont and Fletcher and Shakespeare himself were to develop. The relation of *The Tempest* to *Measure for Measure* is fascinating, but it is an ill-advised criticism that would suppose this play to be explained as a premature attempt at what Shakespeare achieved in the late romances.[6] In sum, labeling the play "tragicomedy" solves nothing and is rather more inexact and misleading than calling it a "problem" play. The truth of the matter is that *Measure for Measure* is unique. There is nothing really like it in all the Elizabethan drama, including the rest of Shakespeare. If ever we are tempted to forget how experimental a playwright Shakespeare was, *Measure for Measure* is there to remind us.

If there is a beginning of anything like wisdom about this play it has to be here; and we must set out from it with due acknowledgement of the sort of dramatist the experimenter was at this point in his career. *Hamlet,* and *Twelfth Night* too, concluding the romantic comedies, were behind him; he must have had *Othello* in progress when he attempted this play; and a year hence he was to produce *King Lear.* Shakespeare was in mature possession of still-developing powers and well advanced in the profoundest exploration of tragedy ever achieved. That fact makes some critical propositions patently dubious, among them the notion that "the first half of *Measure for Measure* has the dramatic impact of a play comparable to *Hamlet*," whose expected and proper tragic consequence Shakespeare ruinously thwarts when he "shifts his dramatic emphasis in the direction of comedy and intrigue."[7] Even before turning to evidence that shows this assertion mistaken, we can find it preposterous in its unstated presuppositions about the playwright. We need to remember that *Measure for Measure* stands—along with *Troilus and Cressida*—as the most self-consciously intellectual of Shakespeare's plays. Indeed, if *Measure for Measure* does prove a failure, it will not be as an aborted tragedy, but as a play climactically sequent upon the two experimental plays immediately preceding it in this period of Shakespeare's creativity.[8]

Troilus and Cressida and *All's Well that Ends Well* are different from *Measure for Measure* and from each other, but they share a highly self-conscious interest in radically manipulating expectations of kind and, relatedly, complexities of ironic perspective. Through a relentless analysis of action in relation to disordered value, *Troilus* develops intensively the idea of an anticlimactic structure that Shakespeare had advanced in *Richard II*. Strong generic reference is made to the heroic and the romantically tragic, and not without complication of the tone; but *Troilus*'s insistent effect is ironically to expose the incapacity for such action in a world diseased and disordered where the forms of appetite actually rule under other names. Along with the praiser, praise, and praised, this play about frustration—about impotence and dissolution both—deflates every pretense to ideality in desire, choice, and action, in selfhood as in civilization. The energetic and searching comic-satyric irony places the audience at a critical and intellectual distance, where it can enjoy the exhilaration of participating in perceptive art's clarifying order about a disordered world.

But this distanced view is unstable and precarious for two dramatically calculated reasons. Yearning for the completing idealities denied by the exposure, we would dissociate ourselves from Thersites' degrading assessments. On the other hand, the irony attacks the audience. The "broken music" is to be heard in its world, and the discord from that "untuned string" as well.[9] Since we do not live "in the peace and married calm of states," the inner and outer wars of the play adumbrate ours, along with the romanticizing of appetite, deflatable language, and debunkable reason. Ulysses' famous speech on degree, as it is addressed to the Greek council, appropriately omits God to authorize and sustain universal order. Depicted is a world where it is left to man to see and sustain it. Does that for the audience comfortingly distinguish its world, or make an ironic comment upon it?

Certainly Ulysses' and Hector's counsels make paradigms uncomfortably close to the bone. One would employ the root cause of the disorder he has diagnosed as politic means to win the victory disorder has denied. The other justifies, in the name of honor, persistence in a course he sees "right reason" must find wrong. The audience shares that "one touch of nature [which] makes the whole world kin"; by the operations of that nature, our moment-bound and sense-drawn misdeemings make "degree vizarded," thus conspiring with "envious and calumniating Time" to undo value (I.iii.83–84; III.iii.170ff.). All this reaches to the Epilogue, as in *Twelfth Night* the actual conclusion (of certainly one version) of the play, where Pandarus on its behalf would bequeath to the "traders in the flesh" in the audience the diseases already daily contracted from the galled Winchester geese. The effect of this play by its close, if complex in tone, is strangely invigorating and clarifying, which no one (I think) has yet said of the conclusion of *Measure for Measure*. Yet the later is related to the earlier play more closely than has been acknowledged.

In *All's Well that Ends Well,* further probing the themes of worth and honor and the relation between word and deed, Shakespeare dares to conjoin opposite ends of the spectrum of comedy, irony, and romance. He does two other accordant remarkable things. He inverts comedy's usual generational arrangements by having the elders (associated with a better past) promote the match of the young couple, and he has the main obstacle to their union be the husband elected by the romantic heroine, a proud and callow "noble" youth who refuses to acknowledge the wife he is forced to marry. Shakespeare ends the comedy by using the folk-motif of the bed-trick to complete the exposure of the young husband— who is carefully shown not to have changed essentially at all—and yet to fulfill the fairy-tale conditions whose satisfaction, talismans and all, compel him to acknowledge his wife and take her to his promised love. This ending also deliberately (as Ann Barton has said) forces "a clash between those opposing elements of fairy tale and realism, of romance motivation and psychological probability which have existed in so uneasy a harmony throughout." *All's Well* has literally the most "if"-peppered comic ending in Shakespeare, who knew there to be "much virtue in 'if.'" Barton thinks the "kind of pyrrhic victory" which romance wins in the final scene of *All's Well that Ends Well* is disturbing, because it "raise[s] in a particularly acute and deliberate fashion doubts as to the validity of comedy as an image of truth." And she believes romance does this again through the bed-trick in *Measure for Measure* a year later.[10]

All's Well will never be the favorite of Shakespeare's comedies, but it is now properly being more appreciated as the extraordinary mixed venture it is. For Shakespeare, surely, the challenge was to learn from it and top it with a distinctly original play. In fact the bed-trick is very different in *Measure for Measure:* first because the emphasis is on the developed Diana figure, the chaste woman illicitly propositioned for whom a substitute is required, but also because the trick is not as well integrated into the plot as it is in *All's Well.* As Hal Gelb observes, the device to achieve resolution of the action does not arise from the earlier action it resolves.[11] The Mariana plot and the bed-trick are not mentioned until the fifth grouping of III.i, and Mariana first appears at the start of act IV. The mention recasts Angelo. We had not before been asked to think of him as the unloving unworthy beloved. The shift of locale to the moated grange with that lovely song (the only one in the play) fairly fanfares the play's shifted emphasis in apparent premise; but Shakespeare is not trying to get away with anything. He invokes romance and the airs it brings before doing something quite original not in keeping with it.

The arrestingly dreamlike detailed description of the place and circumstance of the rendezvous sorts with the romance context. But it is reported, while Mariana is offstage, to the Friar by Isabella, who has twice been shown the way with the two keys by Angelo. His and Isabella's implication in the psychologically charged meeting arranged is emphasized, as, differently, is the Duke's in the substitution he would contrive.[12] Mariana, who is briefed by Isabella while the Duke soliloquizes, says remarkably little. Even her willingness to undertake the enterprise is expressed by Isabella. And the last note struck is the Duke-Friar's startling assurance that Mariana will not be committing a sin in undertaking it. That emphasis is passing strange for romance; but it advertises considerations elsewhere important in the play which require to be intruded here. Mariana's continuation in her strong love of Angelo despite his "unjust unkindness" is of course never further explained than when first remarked in III.i; it is a given, though covered as such by being remarked as strange. But in her unveiled confrontation of "cruel Angelo" and her plea for his life in the final scene, romantic in itself, that love achieves an urgently realistic incarnation.

What we are talking about is a generic reference to romance in a contrasting context which the audience is invited to witness in just those terms. The play issues no carte blanche to invoke uninhibitedly our notions of the whole order of romance. Northrop Frye once wrote that "the problem in *Measure for Measure* is how Isabella's chastity, always a magical force in romance, is going to rescue both the violated Julietta and the jilted Mariana as a result of being exposed to the solicitations of Angelo."[13] That is very ingenious, but it is not by Isabella's chastity or Isabella herself that Julietta—for which, to take the play's emphasis, read Claudio—or Mariana is rescued. In fact a loss of chastity is required. If there is any magical force, it is in the continuing love of Mariana. But this play does not delineate it as magical. Romance is not in position to win a pyrrhic victory in the final scene of *Measure for Measure;* the aegis and decreer of the finale is the Duke.

The play also makes generic reference to tragedy—a fact that has been the root of such revealing confusion that it is worth considering in some detail. One could take some version of the characters and essential situations of Claudio, Angelo, and Isabella and make some sort of tragedy out of it all, but Shakespeare's address to the "monstrous ransom" story shows no such inclination. It simply is untrue that Shakespeare "begins" in III.i to turn a tragic *action* to comedy. That is a fiction begotten by critical argument; it never happened. Shakespeare's conjunction of the ruler-in-disguise motif with the monstrous ransom story implies a comic direction, and that demonstrably is an initiating, not a late, idea in the creative process. Everything we know of Shakespeare's principal alterations of his sources indicates circumvention of tragic formulation or resolution of his play. These changes testify to what Richard Blackmur used to call "executive decisions" by the writer, and one would expect so humble a creature as a critic to follow Shakespeare's not doing what he plainly had no intention of doing. That is not to deny the deepening darkness of Angelo's corrupting with virtuous reason, the cruel pain of the extortive tests Isabella undergoes, or the terror of Claudio's apprehension of death and the humiliating abasement of his plea to live. There is matter in the play to test the reach of any proposed comic purgation. But those who would have us suppose that "the first half of the play" is a tragic action thwarted by Shakespeare's turning to comedy and intrigue in the second do not tell us that the gripping dialogues in the first half *propose* irreversible actions that are not performed, or, as is the case with Claudio's plea to his sister and her furious rejection of him, perform actions that are immediately qualified. Scourged by her passionately overdetermined denial and stiffened to be absolute for death by the Duke's disinformation about Angelo's test of her, Claudio begs her forgiveness, in pantomime, twenty lines after her turning from his "But hear me, Isabel."

Herbert Weil speaks for those who think that a critic of *Measure for Measure* has no right to "add stage business that reconciles Isabella to Claudio, thereby violating both her bitter vituperation and her striking silence to him after the last lines she speaks to her brother."[14] He is mistaken. "Let me ask my sister's pardon," addressed to the Friar, the only authority known by Claudio to be onstage, requires the action it describes in advance. The Duke's summoning of the Provost, concealed onstage, to ask him to exit provides the covering routine. During it Claudio and Isabella are both onstage. What are they to do, shift from leg to leg and ignore one another? Often you can confirm what has to be in a play by what would happen if you omitted it; for Shakespeare, first of all, had to do so. If there is no reconciliation here, an audience must be puzzled by the lack of one later, when the living Claudio is produced for the denouement, and where text and action quickly require its attention to be otherwise preoccupied.

That mimed reconciliation occurs before the shift in the play with the Duke's proposal of his "remedy." On the other hand, those who posit a "tragic first half" do not tell us that Angelo's most heinous *deed*—his treacherous ordering of Claudio's execution—is entirely a matter of the so-called "second half" of the play. That deed is not represented directly, as in tragedy, with Angelo before us, but through the efforts to contravene his written order. But it does produce one consequential speech in itself tragic, when Angelo's pained conscience makes him wish Claudio had lived.

> He should have liv'd;
> Save that his riotous youth, with dangerous sense,
> Might in the times to come have ta'en revenge
> By so receiving a dishonour'd life
> With ransom of such shame. Would yet he had lived.
> Alack, when once our grace we have forgot,
> Nothing goes right; we would, and we would not.   [*Exit.*]
>
> (IV.iv.26–32)

Angelo in soliloquy realizes his trapped spiritual state. That state, though reversible, and even though we know Claudio is not dead and the context is bustling with preparation for his grace the Duke's return, is quite real.

If the "first half" presents a play of the order of *Hamlet,* we should be able to say what tragic situation is then supposedly betrayed. But before the Duke proposes his too-good-to-refuse plan and tells of Mariana, the play itself summarizes the situation "as the matter now stands" (III.i.194–95). We have a Claudio who has begged his sister's pardon and is "so out of love with life that I will sue to be rid of it," encouraged by a most unconfessorlike Friar to hold himself in that view awaiting execution. Next, we have an Isabella who conclusively affirms, "I had rather my brother die by the law, than my son should be unlawfully born" (188–90). And finally, there is a considered Angelo—a character surely not the size of a tragic hero, the very economics of whose heart are wrong for such a role. He is to be left refused in his foul demand, uncontented in his discovered lust, but also able to escape Isabella's determination to accuse him. "Yet, as the matter now stands, he will avoid your accusation—he made trial of you only" (194–96). Where are those implicit terrible consequences whose working out Shakespeare's turn to comedy has prevented, thus making his play (as Harriet Hawkins once dared to call it) "a festered lily"?[15] In ironic fact, it is the putting in practice of the Duke's remedy in the play's "second half" that produces, and plainly more than the Duke intends it to produce, deeds capable of making many writers on the play feel Angelo unworthy of a place in a comic resolution. Hawkins appears to suppose that if objection can be lodged against the play's ending as comic resolution, then her notion of its first half as tragic is confirmed. That does not follow. What does follow is that the play's principal generic reference—which is to comedy—may be only that. It also follows that we can place no confidence whatever in such a critic's reading of the "first half" of the play.

The idea that *Measure for Measure* is a tragedy betrayed could never have occurred were it not for two circumstances. First, that the play is puzzling as a whole, bewildering in tonal variety, its very coherence in doubt, has induced a tendency to fragment it, and concentrate the assimilative center of understanding in a preferred view of some major part or aspect of the play. And of course—and here is the second circumstance—Isabella's dialogues with Angelo and then Claudio are stunning. But the latter confrontation is not, as discussions of it would lead us to expect (and as eighteenth-century editors from Pope to Johnson actually made it), a separate scene. It is not even a duologue with those two characters on stage alone. The textual tradition adding an exit for the Duke and Provost at III.i.152, which runs from F2 through the later Folios and from Davenant and Rowe to Evans in the Riverside, is erroneous. In insisting that before the play's "second half" "there is no dramatic insulation between our personal response and characters who arouse in us simultaneous pity and terror,"[16] Hawkins ignores the fact that the Duke, already introduced in the prison with Juliet in the scene preceding the second Isabella-Angelo interview, is onstage placed to overhear the climactic exchange between brother and sister. That is a more serious omission than failing to mention the presence of Lucio and the Provost throughout the first interview of Isabella with Angelo because of the expectation, raised in the play's third scene, that as eiron in his Friar's disguise the Duke will be present to prevent things going wrong. Whatever questioning that role undergoes—and the questioning begins at once—the very story convention invoked "establishes a climate for comedy" (B. Evans),[17] providing a conditioning frame or envelope for the action that follows. And Isabella is not even brought onstage until that frame is in place.

Gelb, who acknowledges the frame but thinks it falls away in the Claudio-Isabella grouping, would add, "Yet this assurance of comedy is introduced only after the audience has experienced the death threat to Claudio as real (I.ii) and only after tragic possibilities have been seeded." What tragic possibilities? The death threat to Claudio is by judicial enforcement of a law that itself alters perception of the threat. The offense of the condemned man, which in Cinthio is rape, Whetstone has altered to the succumbing to the "blynde affects in love" by a young man and his girl. His sister Cassandra, though she calls this a "foule act," nevertheless firmly regards it as the Elizabethan audience obviously was expected to regard it, as an offense whose proper "desart"—and remedy— is marriage.

> For which foule act he is adiudgd, eare long to lose his heade.
> The lawe is so seuere, in scourging fleshly sinne,
> As marriage to worke after mends doth seldome fauor win.
> A law first made of zeale, but wrested much amis.
> Faults should be measured by desart, but all is one in this,
> The lecher fyerd with lust, is punished no more
> Then he which fel through force of loue, whose mariage salues his
>   sore:[18]

Shakespeare's changes are striking. No one in his Vienna challenges the justice of the law itself. No one in the play comments on the inequity the audience is left to observe, that bawds and pimps go free while a young man is condemned to death. And Shakespeare's young offender arguably is (at least with reference to English common law) legally married. Claudio's offense is unsanctioned intercourse before properly consented wedlock and solemnization of marriage. These changes liberate an audience to feel—at the level of literal apprehension—that the secular law by which he is condemned to death, though a *donnée* of the play world, is so outrageously severe as to be sorted with those arbitrary laws that comedy is expected to circumvent.

As to the suspense generated by Claudio's situation, it is aimed by the close of that second scene through the placing of his hopes, in the Duke's absence, on his sister's intercession with his deputy. What immediately follows in the audience's experience is such doubtful warrant of Claudio's safety as can be found in the Duke's continued presence in Vienna. It must be doubtful given the Duke's doubts about the deputy he chose in expectation that he would *enforce* the unspecified "most biting laws" which the Duke himself had too leniently neglected. This complication of the import of the Duke's presence in disguise serves to forestall premature closure or facile delimitation of the debate about liberty and restraint.

The Duke in disguise has the corollary effect, as Anthony Caputi observes, of diminishing "long-range melodramatic suspense . . .

in favor of fixing our attention on the moral quality of the action." Given the Duke, we are reasonably certain how things will turn out.

> Instead, we are invited to attend closely and critically to what is happening at the moment in scenes contrived to generate a short-range suspense of their own. The Duke's disguise, accordingly, is yet another part of the general pattern calculated to encourage us to view the separate events of the play critically.[19]

Other closely related features of the dramatic pattern emphasized by Caputi—all drawing "the audience's critical faculty into play"— are the resemblance of scenic design to informal debate or disputation in long, slowly developing scenes accounting for more than half the play; a use of important characters so sporadic and irregular "as to imply unmistakably that character was not [the dramatist's] primary concern" (87); and the use of the lowlife characters throughout the play to dramatize conflict represented more distressfully in the scenes involving Angelo, Isabella, and Claudio. Those scenes we surely do not experience with "sardonic detachment" (Stevenson).[20] But the distribution of focus among the characters, and the attention required by the testing of viewpoints, make it plain that the audience is not at liberty to engage in uninhibited immediacy with the characters. The supposed lack of dramatic insulation from characters who sear themselves into our imaginations as tragic is entirely the product of the critic's isolating view of them—apart from the play's concerns, the demands and effect of its much more complex methods of representation, and the contexts it supplies.

Those dialogues become not only the touchstone but the substance of the play's "first half," as though they comprised an unbroken unit: unpreceded, unfollowed, and with nothing intervening. Whatever (for instance) is to become of comedy in the "first half"? Kemble, in producing the play, obviously wanted to aim it as directly as possible at the first Isabella-Angelo interview (II.ii). Thus, he put the Duke at the monastery (I.iii) right after the opening scene so that the convent scene (I.iv), with Lucio's appeal for Isabella's intercession, would immediately follow the play's second scene and directly precede that interview. However, the Pompey-Elbow-Froth matter, too good (and too popularly stageworthy) to cut, he yet included, though making it follow what it was meant to precede. He stuck it between the two Isabella-Angelo interviews instead of the Duke-Juliet scene (II.iii), which he dropped.[21] But what is a critic like Hawkins, with her hands full of a yet to be aborted tragedy, to do with two prunes "in a fruit dish, a dish of some three pence, your honours have seen such dishes, they are not china dishes, but very good dishes,—"?

Drama is a fleeting, and therefore a highly condensing, a necessarily economic, form of art. Witnessing it, we scan for rhythm and pattern, alert for signals pointing construal, expectation, our abuilding sense of the terms of ordering, attentive to qualification and shifts of emphasis or perspective. Above all, we expect and are poised to perceive relationship, through which alone meaning can be conceived. These elementary considerations are hugely important, given Shakespeare's predilection for stretching what dramatic unity might include, and thereby be used to discover, through the often discordant variety he compasses. In this play he takes up a much profounder, and more sophisticated, challenge in this regard than, say, in his earlier triumph *A Midsummer Night's Dream*. But the essential question remains the same: "How shall we find the concord of this discord?" For criticism, that means obligatory continuous concern with the conditions of inclusion—of anything and everything—not only in the play but at a particular point, and context, of its unfolding. Shakespeare may put us at our apparent ease, but there is no room for excrescence. What Shakespeare selects for representation demands that we inquire into the terms of its belonging and impact. What he elects to enjoy expansive treatment we may be sure holds major relevance as well as immediate pleasure and point. Now that scene with Pompey is the longest in the play before III.i, over a hundred lines longer than either of the famous Isabella and Angelo scenes that follow it. To ignore it to preserve the immunity of our reading of parts of the play to which we would prefer to attend is to know better than Shakespeare in having his play as we like it—or as we like not to like it.

Because *Measure for Measure* is a play so fundamentally engaged with contradiction, isolation of matter selected from it in arguing a view of the whole has been the bane of its criticism. What Shakespeare has brought together it is self-defeating of us to put asunder, however strange the marriage. That the failure to inquire into the terms of the matter's belonging is a tap root of the problem is clear from the scholar who influentially reformulated the idea that the play is split into two mismatched halves. Tillyard writes of the play's second scene:

In the first half of the play we are in the very thick of action, where different human beings have their own special and different problems and are concerned with how to settle them. Mistress Overdone's problem of what's to be done now all the houses of resort in the suburbs are to be pulled down stands on its own feet quite separate from Claudio's problem of what's to be done now he has been arrested. We are in fact too close to them both to be able to distance them into a single perspective or a common unifying colour.[22]

But all that tells us is that Tillyard did not (or would not) see the single perspective or unifying color. Mistress Overdone and Claudio, both victims of the new enforcement of the vice laws, are in the same scene. Her whole role in the grouping made by her entrance is to tell of Claudio's arrest and sentence for getting Madam Julietta with child; and her bawd's praise of his "worth" to put down the familiar Gentlemen who had just been discussing the diseases purchased by their lechery is pointed mock encomium in advance of his entrance and admission, at Lucio's prompting, that his offense can be called "lechery." At his entry, Pompey, before he tells Madame Mitigation of her profession's plight and survival, repeats the preparation in more figurative manner: yon man is carried to prison for "groping for trouts in a peculiar river." However he may color it in being a married man, Claudio is in fact a fornicator. The single perspective Tillyard does not find is in the argument from the start of the scene, about the human proclivity illustrated by the sanctimonious pirate (and, as Rossiter says, by many of *Measure for Measure*'s critics as well[23]): he went to sea with the Ten Commandments, but scrap'd out of the table of the law the one that inconvenienced his worldly purpose. Madame Mitigation is at the center of the scene's sense. There is a technical point about the staging, however, that partly pulls a different way and may have influenced Tillyard's dissociation of Overdone and Claudio. Pompey, once he has identified for us the point of the procession and the three new principals in it, exits with the bawd before the procession takes the stage and Claudio speaks to object to being shown "thus to th'world."

Mis. O. What's to do here, Thomas tapster? Let's withdraw!

> *Enter* Provost [*and*] Officers [*with*] Claudio *and* Juliet,
> Lucio *and* [*the*] *two Gentlemen*.

Pom. Here comes Signior Claudio, led by the Provost to prison:
and there's Madam Juliet.   *Exeunt.*

Cla. Fellow, why dost thou show me thus to th'world?
Bear me to prison, where I am committed.

(I.ii.105–9)

In fact the Folio incorrectly marked a scene iii here.[24] But what Shakespeare has done is a way of separating parts of a scene as much as sequent groupings in the same scene permit. It is a technique that encourages us to see a distinction between Claudio (and Julietta) and the casual frequenters of houses of resort, and to see through it too.[25]

Yet other techniques of separating conjoined parts of a scene have ironically proved all too successful, for they have, in the presence of other factors, encouraged fragmenting of III.i, the crucial scene where the play undoubtedly tacks to a new heading. The portion of the play's action on the premises first offered has run its course so the Duke properly can assess matters "as [they] now stand." The late exposition about Mariana and Angelo issued through the Duke does more than open possibilities for the future; it also alters perspective of the past, implicitly qualifying our sense of the Duke's shadowy motives in deputizing Angelo and finally clarifying the "kind of character in [Angelo's] life" that urged his choice of him. But the play's change of course otherwise preoccupies Tillyard. At line 151, when (as he sees it) "the Duke enters to interrupt the passionate conversation between Claudio and Isabella" and assumes a role of "guide and controller" not exercised before, Tillyard finds that the play, up to then "predominantly poetical," betrays that it "is not of a piece but changes its nature halfway through."[26] In fact the Duke does not interrupt the passionate conversation of brother and sister; as far as Isabella is concerned, it is over with and done. And the Duke does not even enter at line 151. He merely comes forward from where he eavesdropped, having been onstage (though surely hidden?) since before Isabella's entrance in this prison scene—where, as Friar, he has been guiding Claudio as he earlier, in II.iii, guided Juliet.

But there certainly is change in the scene at the Duke's intervention, marked by a shift to prose. And it is true that from this point
verse no longer predominates, as it had earlier in the play; it is
also true that the best of it, as poetry, does "not touch the great
things in the early part of the play." But the question stifled is
whether this discernment of what is "poetical," so abstracted from
close consideration of its dramatic use, can properly serve as measure of "the nature of the play." Tillyard's kind of attention to the
play is hardly reassuring since he does not see the challenge to his
critical stance in the very scene before him. He thinks whatever
success onstage the play's second half can have is principally due
to such prose comedy as in the Duke's being forced to hear
"Lucio's scandalous remarks on his character in III.2."[27] But there
is no III.ii in the play. Though many writers on *Measure for Measure* (including Caputi, who writes on its scenic design) refer to III.ii
as if it were substantial, it is in fact a phantom. That designation of
a separate scene is an editorial mistake become a tradition because
our reference works are keyed to it. At Isabella's exit the Duke
remains onstage, and Elbow with the arrested Pompey in tow enters to him as the sustainer of the prison locale and to his attempt
to expostulate in verse on the repulsive wickedness of Pompey's
stinking means of livelihood.

Isab.   I thank you for this comfort. Fare you well, good
           father.

                                                              Exit.

                                                             [III.ii]
                Enter Elbow [*and*] *Officers* [*with*] *Pompey.*

Elbow. Nay, if there be no remedy for it, but that you will needs buy
         and sell men and women like beasts, we shall have all the
         world drink brown and white bastard.

Duke. O heavens, what stuff is here!

                                            (III.i.269–70; ii.1–5)

This new grouping plainly is germane to the remedy the Duke
proposed to Isabella before her exit to begin effecting it. It is the
first of no less than seven distinct groupings following her exit that
are part of the same scene, the longest in the play before the finale.
We can hardly claim to be critical of Shakespeare if we ignore the
dramaturgical units in which he works. In sum, Tillyard asserts

that the prose comedy of the play's second half, "excellent though it is, cannot be held consistent with the high poetry of the first half," while he ignores the fact that Shakespeare holds them consistent enough to conjoin them in the very scene where the critic finds that the play splits into irreconcilable halves.[28] The "poetical" confrontation of Isabella and Claudio in fact is contained within a scene that begins and ends with the Duke. He is the character onstage throughout the scene; it features him.

Specialization must not lead us to suppose that the point here concerns a technicality—to be dismissably left to those interested in Jacobean staging, while the play's critics loftily attend to matters of suitable import. The point goes to the heart of the matter. This is a thoughtful play; and a scene is a unit and instrument of thought in representation. But when we turn to *Measure for Measure* criticism, we find the sharp argument about the Duke's counsel to Claudio ("Be absolute for death") dissociated in practice even from Claudio and his sister's memorable confrontation. The audience's awareness of the Duke and Provost's hidden presence onstage simply does not register in discussions of the Isabella-Claudio "scene." Both the Duke's counsel and Isabella and Claudio's dialogue are separated by the "split" in the play from the Duke's proposed remedy; and all that follows in the scene generally is regarded as though it occurred elsewhere and were not part of the same scene. Wherever it is to be found, a truer critical measure for *Measure for Measure* cannot lie that way.

* * *

Measure for Measure at its opening announces itself to be a play about "the properties of government." Consideration moves from the relation of knowledge and action to the obligation of those called to bear responsibility of rule by way of two focal questions. Is there any one of worth to undergo the ample grace and honor of being the substitute for absent true authority? And, what "figure" of it will he bear? The wide net of allusion so gracefully cast by the Duke in his speech to Angelo, urging his virtues to go forth from him in public action, assumes that this commonplace Renaissance exhortation (*Quod in te, prome*) will be seen in the large contextualizing terms (conjoining Christian and Aristotelian-Senecan traditions) of heaven's purpose in bestowing its light, and the investing goddess nature's expectation of thanks and use for lending "the smallest scruple of her excellence." The "figure" image, so familiar in Elizabethan treatments of the ruler as God's vice-regent and resemblance on earth, is picked up implicitly through the assay aspect of the potentially ironic "Spirits are not finely touch'd / But to fine issues" (I.i.35–36), and then explicitly developed as coinage image in Angelo's self-deprecating hesitation to accept his awesome commission.

> *Ang.*   Now, good my lord,
>   Let there be some more test made of my metal,
>   Before so noble and so great a figure
>   Be stamp'd upon it.
> *Duke.*   No more evasion.
>   (47–50)

But the test of his mettle, the Duke insists, will be of man empowered in God-like role. To be assayed, gold is not only "touch'd" but tried in the fire. That is what "test" literally means: namely, cuppled (cf. "tested gold" at II.ii.150). The audience is fairly prepared to expect Angelo to be tested by temptation as a man in his great office. Later in the play the image of the figure-stamped coin will be applied to everyman. (To Angelo, illegitimately begotten children are counterfeits, coinings of "heaven's image / In stamps that are forbid" [II.iv.45–46]). But the context here already insists that the ruler, the substitute in power, "Dress'd" (as Isabella will say) "in a little brief authority"—for all his being thought "'the great Image of God'"—[29] is but the limiting case revealing every man's situation: for everyman is a responsible substitute bearing the figure of God, though all too typically "Most ignorant of what he's most assur'd— / His glassy essence" (II.ii.120–21). The theme of government is analogical. The rule as substitute to which Angelo is called is God-like judgment, but very much on earth: "Mortality and mercy in Vienna / Live in thy tongue, and heart." Given "all the organs / Of our own power," his "scope" is to be as is the Duke's own, but that is "so to enforce or qualify the laws / As to your soul seems good" (44–45; 64–66).

Angelo is precisely presented as the deputy elected by the lord to rule over the earthly city in his stead (17–21). But this charged representation of the choice and empowering of God's substitute, with the Duke going off alone on his mysterious "business" to be a kind of *deus absconditus* but expected to return and (it is hinted) to judge, so far from being an allegory, is symbolic literal enactment[30] inescapably tinged with irony. The Duke's response to Angelo's diffidence about accepting his commission—"No more evasion"—is as ironic at his own expense as his failure to apply to himself all those dicta about the obligations laid on "us" to use the gifts of heaven and nature. As Prince he *is* the deputy elected by the Lord. His uses of personal pronouns are set off as compliments by his notable use of regal ones—until he says farewell (58); thenceforth his pronouns all are personal. His evasion with the excuse of haste of his subject-appointees' desire to bring him something on the way, his explaining "I'll privily away" by his aversion to staging himself to the people's eyes, and his dislike of their "aves vehement"—none of this begins to assuage what it serves to emphasize, the shock of his exit alone. He has imposed on Angelo the role divinely imposed on himself, and the sharp claim of his exit, that the private man can be separated from his public role, is understood to be untenable. That understanding conditions our perspective on the role Angelo is to play, as other odd features of this scene doubly focused on the Duke and Angelo have conditioned it. The Duke initially lauds old Escalus's knowledge and experience of government, gives him a commission, but then makes clear that this paragon (whose onstage presence could have passed for Good Counsel in an earlier play) is not the one he has chosen to rule in his absence. And if Angelo is to have "all the organs of our own power," why does the Duke formally commission a "secondary"? At his exit his two appointees understandably withdraw to look into "the strength and nature" of the power they have. The action will do that too. The scene also implicitly promises that the apparent contradiction, between the Duke's abdicative conduct and the expectation of a parabolic action engendered by allusive reference, ultimately will be clarified.

The crosscut is to an adumbration of the city-world to be governed and thence to the effects of Angelo's new regime. The air of topicality Shakespeare contrives for the gallants' seeming-shallow badinage and the bawd's soliloquized complaint suggests immediate reference in the issues defined for the story; but the subjects touched—politics and war, lechery and venereal disease—are by no accident the paradigmatic ones treated extensively in *Troilus and Cressida*. But to these Shakespeare has added, as the most

inclusive subject, religion. The Gentlemen know God's commandments, but like "the sanctimonious pirate" raze from the table
those forbidding what their appetites and worldly functions require.
They are aware of grace which (as every child had to know at
confirmation) everyman needs because our "captive" corrupt nature is unable to obey the commandments; but what is tauntingly
said to one could be literally said of them all: "thou thyself art a
wicked villain despite of all grace." Grace offers divine mitigation
of man's offenses and of the very inclination to offend against
God's law. But the mitigation they seek is of the stings and motions
of the flesh. Lechery as the symbolic type of "the lusts of the flesh"
in a theological sense is what they are naturally and literally given
to, with the consequence that they can mock each other (at the
considerable length that so disgusted many nineteenth-century
readers) with being diseased. It is not just venereal disease that
has made them sound only as hollow things are sound: "Impiety
has made a feast of thee" (53). The grace they familiarly greet is
"Madame Mitigation," the bawd, herself diseased, under whose
roof their dolors may be purchased.

In this context we hear not only of Claudio's arrest but, after
Lucio and the Gentlemen's interested exit, of Pompey's assurance
of the continuance of Madame Mitigation's trade despite the rigorous proclamation. The houses in the city were to have been pulled
down like those in the suburbs, "but that a wise burgher put in for
them" (91–92)—interceded for them and made a bid to own them.
Pompey enunciates with oracular (and obscene) completeness the
sum of that story: "They shall stand for seed." Pompey's climactic
speech is his bravura reassurance to the bawd, rising to mock emotion, that such devoted public service as hers need not fear destitu-
tion and oblivion by discontinuance of their trade.

> *Pom.* Come: fear not you: good counsellors lack no clients: though
> you change your place, you need not change your trade: I'll
> be your tapster still; courage, there will be pity taken on you;
> you that have worn your eyes almost out in the service, you
> will be considered.
>
> (98–103)

So winning an argument for the value of the disreputable almost
justifies its own inclusion. But in fact here is the first voicing of a

point later iterated, and bound to be given a human proclivity not likely to be extirpated by edict, as Pompey and Lucio will insist. And it will be differently applicable to Claudio too, as the kindly Provost will think him more fit to commit another such offense as die for this one he has committed. Pompey's speech is at once followed by the coming of the procession carrying Claudio and Julietta to prison. But its import carries over to color the Claudio part of the scene, despite the shift to more serious character and his verse, because of the expectation of pertinence in the one scene, because of the usually reflective relation of comic to serious character, but especially because of the framework in which Claudio himself insists that his offense be seen.

> *Cla.*   Fellow, why dost thou show me thus to th'world?
>   Bear me to prison, where I am committed.
>
> *Pro.*   I do it not in evil disposition,
>   But from Lord Angelo by special charge.
>
> *Cla.*   Thus can the demi-god, Authority,
>   Make us pay down for our offence by weight.
>   The words of heaven; on whom it will, it will;
>   On whom it will not, so; yet still 'tis just.
>
>   (108–115)

The shame of Claudio's being "shown to th' world" at Angelo's special charge evinces from him an equivocal speech of the kind that Rossiter finds the play full of, "where there is no resolving the ambiguities, since both meanings 'belong' in the play-frame."[31] He sees the allusion to Romans (ix.15; and see also 18). By this Claudio perceives that the unmitigated weight of justice exacted by "the demi-god Authority" can be paired with the unassailable Justice of God, who shows mercy only to those whom He will, yet always is just. But Rossiter thinks "'yet still 'tis just' can equally be Claudio's bitter comment that Authority can order these needless shames once you are in its hands: and 'it is all called *just.*'" Curiously, a leading proponent of "ambivalence" finds the playwright Shakespeare asking the impossible of the performer: "No actor can play contrite resignation and angry bitterness at once."[32] But the actor must not deliver the glumly bemused "yet still 'tis just" simply as bitter complaint lest he render unplayable his next speech, in which the prisoner explains that his restraint comes "from too much Liberty" (118). Nor, though he acknowledges his offense, can Claudio be regarded as either contrite or as yet resigned. Not until Claudio's third long speech do we get a clear note of self-justification with his recital of the mitigating circumstance, and not until his longest speech the 'why me?' self-exculpating anger at the deputy's tyrannically awakening "me"—the dative of interest—old neglected penalties to make himself "a name" (145–60). But the ambivalence already is deeply marked in the speech in which he speaks "so wisely" about restraint as the consequence of "the immoderate use" of scope. He ends by darkly objecting that we should die for the evil that our natures themselves lead us thirstily to pursue.

> *Lucio.* Why, how now, Claudio? Whence comes this restraint?
>
> *Cla.* From too much liberty, my Lucio. Liberty,
> As surfeit, is the father of much fast;
> So every scope by the immoderate use
> Turns to restraint. Our natures do pursue,
> Like rats that ravin down their proper bane,
> A thirsty evil; and when we drink, we die.
>
> (116–22)

L. C. Knights saw a confusion in the likeness between the two-stepped process of arsenical rat poisoning and the single process of the lecherous thirsty evil.[33] But the "proper bane" is the liberty our natures take as the license to indulge appetite. The resentfully smoldering complaint is not that we are innocent but that we are bound to prove guilty and die for it; and it is not aimed at substitute demi-god authority but at the ratkillerlike Authority under Whose rule we have such a nature. But it is man in bonds, literally "captive," a prisoner, who utters such a complaint.

To make the promise of the continuation of life we expect romantic comedy's young hero to fulfill *after* its end into an unwanted pregnancy that condemns such a character to death at a comic action's start is a very witty idea. Shakespeare makes the wit profound by his treatment of the legal vulnerability under which the character is condemned. Vienna's neglected old law itself is (as A. D. Nuttall says) part of the *story*.[34] The mistake is then to suppose with Rossiter that it "is completely Gilbertian" and thereby to be led to a blinding half truth about the representation: "unless the characters are represented very realistically, the absurdity will make the whole thing a fantasy."[35] The thing is kept from being mere fantasy not simply by realistic characterization but by basing the fantasy on a deeper "realism" than Rossiter considers. The "what if" of the fantasy about secular law is based on the supposition of our actual vulnerability under divine law. The play's situation and emphases compel realization that Claudio is worthy of death under God's law. *Stipendium peccati mors est.* Shakespeare writes here directly in the powerful tradition in which Man's typical sin, sometimes represented literally in pictorial iconography, is "fornication."[36] In Shakespeare's representation, symbolic literal enactment in this tradition is an essential aspect of Claudio's dramatic situation. That will assure special point to every effort to find a remedy for his predicament, starting with the "great hope" Claudio has in his sister's intercession with the new deputy.

Of course, many would disagree that Claudio has sinned; but the Duke-Friar, Juliet, and Isabella, later in the play, are explicit that he has. That fact should belatedly warn us that Claudio's centrally placed explanation to Lucio of how it stands with him needs more attentive and informed consideration as dramatic speech. In a play that so emphasizes contradiction between secular and religious viewpoints, it must signify that Claudio does not even address the question of sin. That speech cannot have been meant, and shows it is not, to be construed to be as exculpatory as the speaker intends.

> *Cla.*   Thus stands it with me: upon a true contract
> I got possession of Julietta's bed.
> You know the lady; she is fast my wife,
> Save that we do the denunciation lack
> Of outward order. This we came not to
> Only for propagation of a dower
> Remaining in the coffer of her friends,
> From whom we thought it meet to hide our love
> Till time had made them for us. But it chances
> The stealth of our most mutual entertainment
> With character too gross is writ on Juliet.
>
> (134–44)

To be sure, the play complicates our responses to the matter, not just with that crazy law revived in Vienna, but with the mutuality of the young couple's love, and above all the binding nature of the "true contract" that makes them man and wife. The last has been discussed. Shakespeare exploits the fact that this contract, a *Sponsalia per verba de praesenti,* is being entertained by an English audience while imagined to have occurred in a Catholic circumstance, which is distinctly indicated but twenty-three lines later and driven home by two immediately sequent scenes with conventual settings. At the Council of Trent the Catholic church forbade this form of marriage. In England, where its validity stood in common law, it was widely recognized that such contracts were much abused; churchmen insisted that they be confirmed, not just by "the denunciation of outward order" (the banns), but "with all convenient speed" by church marriage (Hooper). Claudio (like many another) took the contract as warrant to bed the bride; but Lever is doubtless correct to say that "in the view of churchmen, any kind of sexual relationship before a fully consecrated marriage was, of course, sinful" (lv). Moreover, there is more to the matter than that. In Claudio's speech, equal emphasis is placed on the secrecy of their union and the motive for keeping it hidden while they enjoyed their most mutual entertainment. They kept their relationship secret in the hope that relatives who controlled the dowry, and who for some reason did not approve of the match, could be brought around to be "for" them.

In the marriage service in the Book of Common Prayer there is a section devoted to "the entering" into matrimony. Religious and socioreligious writers from the reformers on have much to say on this subject, and if there is anything on which they all agree it is that it is a "pollution" of the entrance into the state of matrimony (Dod and Cleaver) for the young to marry "without consent of parents, or such as are instead of parents" (Sandys). Those "friends" who have Julietta's dowry in trust stand *in loco parentis.* "The children, which presume to marry without the counsel of their parents, do greatly offend God" (Becon). They are not on their own to make "privy contracts" (Latimer); they are not even to "entangle themselves with the love of any person, before they have made their parents, tutors, friends, or such as have governance of them, privy of their intent" (Becon). That is required if it is to be said "that they marry in the Lord." Marriage "may be as much dishonoured" by failure in this regard as by those not allowed by the law of God "to come together" (Sandys).[37] Shakespeare was interested in the entering into the state of matrimony.

The marriage service's treatment of it was one of the sources for the beast imagery in *Measure for Measure*. And it is no accident that a marriage without parental consent importantly figures in the other play he wrote in 1604, *Othello*.

Claudio, the worldly young man who kept his marriage private, ironically enough in hope of the "propagation [that is, breeding] of a dower" (139) understandably is concerned about saving his neck; for him, his soul does not come into it—yet. Though writers on the play usually try, one cannot truthfully refer to Claudio's speeches in this scene apart from the counterpoint of Lucio's, with their variously deflative effect. Melodramatic focus on Claudio's urgent case is undone by Lucio's injected realization of his own peril, and that of his cause: "Is lechery so look'd after?" (133) The tension generated by Claudio's anger at the new governor's tyranny is dissipated when Lucio characteristically cannot resist comparing the "tickle state" of Claudio's head with a maidenhead (161–63). This witty smuttiness in prose, which next trivializes "our love" and "the stealth of our most mutual entertainment" to "a game of tick-tack," surrounds Claudio's verse enlisting Lucio to realize his hope of his sister's intercession. In this play of substitutes Claudio tells Lucio,

> Acquaint her with the danger of my state:
> Implore her, in my voice, that she make friends
> To the strict deputy: bid herself assay him.
> I have great hope in that.
>
> (169–72)

But Claudio's voice, in dramatic preparation for that "assay" of the strict deputy by the would-be novice, speaks of his sister's persuasive powers first in equivocal terms suggesting sexual provocation: "For in her youth / There is a prone and speechless dialect / Such as move men" (172–74). Lucio is fully responsive in answer to this by undertaking his mission to her as much in the prayer that her persuasiveness will free like offense from accusation as to keep his friend's enjoyable life from being "foolishly lost at a game of tick-tack" (177–81). There is not so great a gulf as might appear separating Claudio from "you need not change your trade. I'll be your tapster still. Courage, there will be pity taken on you." But the future is needed to give form to what is here promising suggestion.

The next two scenes are paired in that both have monastic settings, but promise movement back into the world; and both emphasize denial and repression of the power of "love." Our hunger for clarification of the Duke tightly focuses attention at the opening of I.iii on his dismissal of the idea that his purpose in desiring "secret harbour" in the locale defined by Friar Thomas has anything to do with "the aims and ends / Of burning youth" (1–6). Expected ambivalence about the setting implicitly is acknowledged and controlled even as a dramatic promise is made in the Duke's protest at the outset at his "holy father's" thought:

> *Enter* Duke and Friar Thomas.
> *Duke.* No. Holy father, throw away that thought;
> Believe not that the dribbling dart of love
> Can pierce a complete bosom.
>
> (1–3)

The shift from the previous scene in the sterilized conventional language used to refer to love catches attention. And in the language of comedy those who announce their superiority or immunity to love are revealed self-ignorant and are bound to discover its power. The love the Duke confesses is for "the life remov'd" (8). Yet that is not the explanation of his being here either. He tells of turning his power over to Lord Angelo, who now is specifically characterized—"A man of stricture and firm abstinence"—and then teases: "You will demand of me, why I do this" (11–17). But his answer addresses the license encouraged by failure to execute the "strict statutes and most biting laws" that his rule "let slip" though they are "needful bits and curbs to headstrong jades"—the ubiquitous Renaissance symbol for the appetites and passions, most particularly lust, requiring "government."

> *Duke.* We have strict statutes and most biting laws,
> The needful bits and curbs to headstrong jades,
> Which for this fourteen years we have let slip;
> Even like an o'er-grown lion in a cave
> That goes not out to prey. Now, as fond fathers,
> Having bound up the threatening twigs of birch,
> Only to stick it in their children's sight
> For terror, not to use, in time the rod
> Becomes more mock'd than fear'd: so our decrees,

Dead to infliction, to themselves are dead,
And Liberty plucks Justice by the nose,
The baby beats the nurse, and quite athwart
Goes all decorum.

(19–31)

This speech is a very assured and accomplished enlivening of
point by commonplace: the Aesopian lion sorted with the parental
rod familiar in political writings and the topos of "the world upside
down." The coolness and comic control belie facile critical parallel-
ing of this speech with Ulysses' on order rent and deracinated;
there is nothing of the specified terrors of that vision of "appetite
an universal wolf." The speech implies interest in a decorum that
would work. And he explains he has therefore, like a sensible and
politic prince concerned to protect the ducal authority from being
slandered with tyranny, "impos'd the office" of striking home on
the man of stricture, Angelo. So far so clear. But now the same
politic prince wants to behold Angelo's sway disguised in habit
and outward behaviors "like a true friar"—a disguise that *as a
disguise* is by this time quite traditionally ironic.[38] The "more reasons for this action" he will share with Friar Thomas we of course
are denied, but the Duke arrests us with "Only this one:"

Lord Angelo is precise;
Stands at a guard with Envy; scarce confesses
That his blood flows; or that his appetite
Is more to bread than stone. Hence shall we see
If power change purpose, what our seemers be.

Exeunt.
(50–54)

One may well ask whether hence we shall see, "If power change
seeming, what our purposes be." But I think the audience (though
as aware of the question as the critics who worry it) is expected
to be content to await the disclosure since the Duke *is* telling what
the play has not shown in action but needs to be known if the action
predicted is to be fully enjoyed. It is worth saying immediately that
his performing this function by no means makes him Shakespeare's
spokesman in the action.

"More to bread than stone" is clear as it stands. But the reminis-
cence of Matthew 7:9 (in the Sermon on the Mount to which the

play's title alludes) may be suggestive rather than "a rather vague recollection" (Lever). Jesus is talking about the Father's gifts to His children—a matter crucial to the play from its first scene; and it is obviously pertinent, to any post-Reformation audience (or indeed any audience familiar with comedy), to the repression of natural powers—as the reformers viewed it, a contempt of God's gifts—implicit in the monastic setting of scenes iii and iv.[39] Certainly Angelo is skeptically viewed as presuming a God-like capacity (like Christ's at the Temptation, Matt. 4:3) to be immune to the temptation to fleshly appetite. The precise Angelo's extreme comic vulnerability, which ironically reflects back on the Duke's claim to "a complete bosom," also impinges on the God-like presumption in his own more enigmatic role. Isabella, as she now is introduced at the convent, will prove to be vulnerable on both counts. Imaginatively we receive her in her desire for repression as counterpart to Angelo, but also, as she is drawn back to the world she was to renounce in her religious costume, as parallel to the Duke. Since she is not yet sworn to the role her costume indicates, she can be seen the more readily as in disguise too. That is an idea most subtly developed, for Isabella is a very special experiment in the comedy to be generated by the unconsciousness of the highly conscious.

First impressions count enormously in the theater, and Shakespeare had the idea for a very efficient way of instantly projecting Isabella. The scene catches her accompanied by the nun Francisca—the image of what she would choose to become—at the very threshold of her commitment to her "probation" and in the midst of converse that renews the issue of scope and restraint and brings the prison and the convent into one orbit.

> *Enter* Isabella *and* Francisca *a Nun.*
>
> *Isab.*   And have you nuns no farther privileges?
>
> *Nun.*   Are not these large enough?
>
> *Isab.*   Yes, truly; I speak not as desiring more,
> But rather wishing a more strict restraint
> Upon the sisters stood [sisterhood, F2]; the votarists
>   of Saint Clare.
>
> *Lucio.* [*within.*] Hoa! Peace be in this place!
>
> *Isab.*   Who's that
>   which calls?
>
> *Nun.*   It is a man's voice!
>
> (iv.1–7)

It is as essential for a reader as for a director or performer to ask where a character stands, or places herself, to speak as she does. With her first words Isabella misrepresents herself in that testing inquiry that draws response from Francisca. In effect she creates occasion to declare herself—in all her assured inexperience—as wanting more strictness than a famously austere order practiced. Yet the import is not quite as though she were shopping for the right order or were the Inspector General of Convents, but rather of enthusiasm in naivete about the self. Immediately we have the male voice intruding from the world; this eager earnestness of immature religious enthusiasm is set against Francisca the nun's anxious recitation of the claustrophobic inhibitions and artificial rules about converse with the other sex that she is under and Isabella will be when she has vowed. That she has not yet done so the action emphasizes.

> Gentle Isabella
> Turn the key, and know his business of him;
> You may, I may not; you are yet unsworn:
>
> (7–9)

This scene is a nice example of how the means Shakespeare employs to create locale make place really one with action. With the aid of that significant offstage presence, the Prioress—the Mother to whom Isabella exits to give notice of her affair at the close (11; 86)—Francisca the nun (a fine small part) creates the convent. She decorously retires as her rule dictates, but remains onstage, so Lucio is not alone with Isabella, and so we have that counterpoise to him to create the scene he is in with Isabella. He comes as the very embodiment of scope for everything in human nature the convent's rules, strictures, locks are fearfully arrayed against. He makes an entrance like a joke that Shakespeare makes it seem the character couldn't resist. Having been admitted to the *hortus conclusus* he burlesques the Angel of the Annunciation, turning the *Ave* into a rake's testing flattery of the virgin she appears to be.

Enter Lucio.

Lucio. Hail virgin, if you be—as those cheek-roses
    Proclaim you are no less—can you so stead me
    As bring me to the sight of Isabella,

A novice of this place, and the fair sister
To her unhappy brother Claudio?

(16–20)

She hardly can believe the shameful news she hears from such a
source anymore than we can long uncritically share in his shallow
irreverence. He tries straightfaced flattery mocking with cynical
doubt what she must want to believe of herself.

Lucio.   'Tis true.
    I would not, though 'tis my familiar sin,
    With maids to seem the lapwing, and to jest
    Tongue far from heart, play with all virgins so.
    I hold you as a thing enskied and sainted
    By your renouncement, an immortal spirit,
    And to be talk'd with in sincerity,
    As with a saint.
Isab.   You do blaspheme the good, in mocking me.
Lucio.   Do not believe it.

(30–39)

Amazingly, many Isabelites have taken Lucio's comment straight,
but then again there are actresses who get her response wrong and
make a prig of her. "The good" and "me," as Lever notes, are in
contrast. She sees through him and tells him what he is doing.
That pushes him to get to the point—and here, insuppressibly,
there is a surprise.

                         Fewness and truth; 'tis thus:
    Your brother and his lover have embrac'd;
    As those that feed grow full, as blossoming time
    That from the seedness the bare fallow brings
    To teeming foison, even so her plenteous womb
    Expresseth his full tilth and husbandry.
Isab.   Someone with child by him? My cousin Juliet?
Lucio.   Is she your cousin?
Isab.   Adoptedly, as schoolmaids change their names
    By vain though apt affection.
Lucio.   She it is.

Isab.   O, let him marry her!

(39–49)

His refreshing speech is not shaped out of Lucio's character in a completely incarnative manner. But it ironically places his viewpoint as it yet more emphatically contrasts with the convent and calls it into question. Human generation here is seen to be as natural as eating or the seasons. But this Shakespearean invocation of the order of universal plenitude is made (like Ulysses' famous speech) ironic by the absence of God from his living creation. Thus, between the extremes of the "naturalist" view and the convent we get a glimpse of what is denied by both. Here is the value of making Isabella so very alive in this context by "cousin Juliet"— a most Shakespearean idea. It gives her dimension in human relation and an affective past, though looked at from what she regards as her mature present. But her "O, let him marry her!" is as free and direct as it is wholesome and sensible.

That is Lucio's cue to explain Claudio's predicament, and her exclamation emphasizes his next omission, which is of any reference to Claudio's claim to be married. That is characteristic of Lucio and useful to Shakespeare. For all the ink expended on discussion of marriage *per verba de praesenti* in this play, no one but Claudio in scene ii refers to Claudio's marriage. Shakespeare can thus have, at its introduction, the force of this consideration, and then free the debate to come from such an extenuating particular so that the argument can be as general as possible.

Lucio's review of the situation emphasizes in turn the Duke's absence, his substitute's frigidity and monklike self-repression ("one who . . . doth rebate and blunt his natural edge / With profits of the mind, study and fast"), his rigorous construction of the hideous law to make her brother an example, and her brother's hope residing entirely in the role she is called upon to play (50–71). Knowing that Lucio has come to impose that role on her, the audience is watchful of the terms in which it is presented and her response. The latter is the pendant to Angelo's response to the role imposed on him in scene i, and a nice variation upon it.

> *Isab.*   Alas, what poor ability's in me
>   To do him good!
>
> *Lucio.*   Assay the power you have.
>
> *Isab.*   My power? Alas, I doubt.
>
> *Lucio.*   Our doubts are traitors,

And makes us lose the good we oft might win
By fearing to attempt.

(75–79)

The presentation of the role is subtly contrived to be at once literal and also answerable to the symbolic dimensions of Claudio's dilemma as sinful man whose life "Falls into forfeit." This train of suggestion is lightly continued with a dual preparative touch.

> All hope is gone,
> Unless you have the grace by your fair prayer
> To soften Angelo.
> . . . . . . Go to Lord Angelo,
> And let him learn to know, when maidens sue,
> Men give like gods; but when they weep and kneel,
> All their petitions are as freely theirs
> As they themselves would owe them.

(68–70; 79–83)

Though this play is no allegory, it does play with allegories of its substance. Lucio surely is costumed as a gallant, like the figure of Lechery from the moral plays the drunken Toby reports after seeing Cesario at the gate (*TN* I.v.120). He comes to lead the "thing enskied and sainted" into the world on a mission of mercy given a doubly dubious cast. The writings and sermons of the reformers were as repetitive as adamant that man's only advocate and intercessor with God is Christ, because only He is redemptive mediator (1 John ii:1–2).[40] Catholic beliefs about the Virgin and saints are held as presumptuously erroneous as associated conceptions of monasticism in this regard, for example, that of the *thesaurus* to be drawn on in affecting the afterlife of others. A modern audience readily sees the contrast between Lucio and the convent; but a principal point of the generic reference to antimonastic satire (as Gless has argued[41]) is to expose the irony that at the theological level the convent is as "fleshly" as the worldly defender of license who already in this scene is warming Isabella to her role: "To soften Angelo."

The preparative movement of the play has now extended through four scenes in which focus on character has been calculatedly distributed. All that is needed to give a sense of its completion is to return to Angelo and Escalus, absent through the last three scenes, and exactly fix the strict deputy's position. "We must not make a scarecrow of the law" (II.i.1), the next scene's first theme, is announced at the first by Angelo in the midst of argument repeating Escalus's urging of leniency to Claudio. His focal attempt is to remind Angelo that he himself—"though most straight in virtue"— under the right circumstances could have erred like Claudio "through the resolute acting of our blood" and pulled the law upon himself (8–16). But this dents Angelo's certainty in his judgment— and his consistency in it—not at all. Angelo has not fallen: "'Tis one thing to be tempted, Escalus, / Another to fall" (17–18).

> You may not so extenuate his offence
> For I have had such faults; but rather tell me,
> When I that censure him do so offend,
> Let mine own judgement pattern out my death,
> And nothing come in partial. Sir, he must die.
>
> (27–31)

With this predictive utterance—where dramatic irony is produced by the confident speaker's rhetoric pulling one way while the "when" clause points another—Angelo, left to his wisdom, confirms the order for Claudio's execution and with it the untempered misrule of his government. But Escalus's concluding couplets have the last word; they epigrammatically assess the situation in the large context of all men's need of God's forgiveness and through the paradoxical nature of sin and virtue in the contrasted spheres of His judgment and mercy and man's.

> *Esc.* Well, heaven forgive him; and forgive us all.
> Some rise by sin, and some by virtue fall.
> Some run from brakes of ice and answer none,
> And some condemned for a fault alone.
>
> (37–40)

The last couplet looks at inequity in the blind operation of justice here: he thinks of what Angelo has said "we never think of" (26). If only "what's open made to justice" does it seize upon (21–22), then many deserving of punishment answer to none while some are condemned for a single fault. The second line, because its reference and paradoxes are dual, has the farthest preparative reach. "Some rise by sin, and some by virtue fall"—italicized in the Folio—can speak of the injustice in the fortunes of a fallen world, but it also compressedly addresses the paradoxes of temptation as often discussed in Elizabethan religious writings. Sinning makes some rise, because it teaches them their weakness and their share in everyman's need of God's mercies. Some by virtue fall, because it can blind with proud supposition of sufficiency, because it can be narrowly pursued without reference to the virtue denied by the pursuit, and because it can actually disguise the vice most resembling it. As Angelo will be astonished to find, and as he is used to discover very literally, it is possible to be led to sin in loving virtue.

At this point in the play everything is in place for melodrama in the main narrative to occupy stage center. The engine has been wound and urgencies point to immediate entrance of Isabella for the awaited big scene in which she pleads with Angelo for her brother's life. Instead we get Elbow and Officers with Froth and Pompey for a very different big scene. The four groupings, till they are got offstage, comprise an action far longer than any of the four *scenes* preceding; and that action, like the displacement itself, is comic and deflative. In Shakespeare's arrangement of our experience of his play, this substituted comic hearing of a cause is strategic, conditioning the effect of what ensues; and criticism that comes at the great dialogue of Isabella and Angelo, and its ironic outcome, by any other route subverts Shakespeare. Part of his method here we have been exposed to in the play's second scene, where the early groupings with Lucio, the Gentlemen, and the bawds are used to generate the limelight in which we perceive the Claudio part of the scene. Already we subliminally expect Angelo to be tempted and to fall through "the resolute acting of our blood," and this interlude variously prepares for the next scene, anticipates it, illuminates it in advance, even essentially plays out its action. For in this parody of the morality contest between Justice and Iniquity (II.i.169), the bawd outsmarts and gets the best of deputy justice. Shakespeare even glances at the delay of the oncoming action by this imbroglio to the point of laying the ground for the later play on "your honour." Escalus is climactically demanding that Pompey get to the point.

> *Esc.* Come, you are a tedious fool. To the purpose: what was done
> to Elbow's wife that he hath cause to complain of? Come me
> to what was done to her.

Pom.   Sir, your honour cannot come to that yet.

Esc.   No, sir, nor I mean it not.

Pom.   Sir, but you shall come to it, by your honour's leave.

(115–21)

This interlude is an extraordinary experiment in liberating dramatic expression.

Its remarkable summarizing and referential capability is released by its comic license, abundantly issued at the start by the "poor Duke's constable" (47–48). Elbow "lean[s] upon justice" (48–49). Justice falls down and we laugh. Shakespeare enlists our delighted participation in a triumph of comic anarchy.[42] The atmosphere is infectious. Escalus cannot resist straight-faced solicitous ridicule of Elbow though the quick Pompey must be part of his audience. Even Angelo, before he leaves, gets into the act. Some find his leaving the endlessly tedious hearing "Hoping you'll find cause to whip them all" (133–36) neglectful and cruelly severe. But what better way to exhibit a humorless character, than to have this unsmiling line be his one essay at humor? (See how Shakespeare turns this idea later, at V.i.232: "I did but smile till now.") Escalus is left in charge for his lenient disposition of the judicial hearing that Elbow and Pompey between them subvert. Angelo, who must be got off for his reappearance in the next scene, is not needed onstage while we have Elbow, with his trumpeted knowledge of the law (43), to caricature deputy authority. The next scene will give us Isabella's eloquent portrait of "proud man, / Dress'd in a little brief authority" down to "every pelting petty officer," whose antics "before high heaven" make the angels, who lack our risibility, weep. Here we have the thing itself to make us laugh ourselves mortal.

In the topsy-turvydom seen through Elbow's misplacings, the judges are varlets, Pompey is an honorable man, a respected fellow, indeed (as he himself earlier implied) a benefactor.

Ang.   Benefactors? Well, what benefactors are they? Are they not malefactors?

Elbow.   If it please your honour, I know not well what they are. But precise villains they are, that I am sure of, and void of all profanation in the world, that good Christians ought to have.

(51–56)

Here Elbow's words make sense that finds in the bawd and his customer awaiting service a villainous identity that (as Lever says) ironically comments on Angelo's principles. Through Elbow's misplacings the wise fool speaks. Good Christians cannot be without profanation in the world because they are confessed sinners (all whose goodness comes from God); argal, the precise who are— or claim to be and puritanically would have us be—void of such profanation are villains. We take the point here about the would-be legislators of morality with an understanding akin to that informing our later appreciation of Pompey's suggestion to Escalus: "If your worship will take order for the drabs and the knaves, you need not to fear the bawds" (231–32).

The other deputies, starting with the Duke and Escalus, hardly fare better. The way in which Elbow, whose unsuitability for office reflects on Angelo, got to be the "poor Duke's" officer slyly indicts the Duke: those who were chosen as sufficient to serve duck their responsibility and "are glad to choose me for them" (266). Again, in the judgment of Escalus that permits Pompey to "continue" and the law to prove a mere scarecrow, the too-great leniency for which the Duke reproves his own former rule in the story is exemplified in the action. In the turns of the scene, where it is as though Shakespeare suspended a complex mirror from a twisted string, we get mind-catching reflections too of that everyman deputy-figure Claudio. Mocking Elbow with his own misplacings, Pompey claims the constable's wife (who is great with child) was "respected with him before he married with her" (167–68). But it is the honorable man Pompey, ambiguous tapster and parcel bawd, who like Claudio is up on a morals charge under the new severity.

Pompey's performance as his own defense lawyer, earnestly cooperating in the inquiry into the truth of "what was done to Elbow's wife" with an interminable testimony, through many-branched irrelevancy, to the innocent circumstantial actualities in which the alleged deed was done, is hilarious because he is faithfully describing a brothel and hardly a phrase in his story of two prunes is without sexual reference. Despite Pompey's heroic efforts at obfuscation and distraction, the disengaged air of Froth (a tiny gem of a comic part), and the demonstration from Froth's innocent face that he could have done no harm to Elbow's wife, the story we get in glimpses, that begins with her pregnant longing for stewed prunes and ends with her spitting in the face of Mrs.

Overdone's pimp, is as clear to us as to Escalus.[43] The audience that sides with Pompey is the same one that sees the joke in the fact that Elbow's wife was not drawn into "fornication, adultery, and all uncleanliness" at Mrs. Overdone's "hot house" because she was not "a woman cardinally given" (78–80). Here anticipated, remarkably, is Angelo's arresting words about the frailty of woman to invite Isabella to be a woman, to put on the destined livery. It is most important to remember the startling fact that the only one in the play, in the represented Vienna, who is married is Elbow. And with that there is a newly enforced law against fornication! Of course the play must carry the characters—including the Duke—toward the imposition of marriage.

Meanwhile, Pompey, like comedy, is a "means" to bring man and woman sexually together. That is the need of our nature and the promise of its continuance. And that promise comedy fundamentally celebrates. All of us are poor fellows who would live and at bottom wish ourselves no other sentence than that which falls on Pompey: "Thou art to continue now, thou varlet, thou art to continue" (188–89). Shakespeare makes us experience the indulgence of license against mocked authority and repressive regulation deeply radical to comedy. The youth of the city will to't; no law, nothing less than gelding and spaying, will change that. We are never more with Pompey than when he challenges the "pretty orders beginning" that call for heading and hanging:

> *Pom.* If you head and hang all that offend that way but for ten year together, you'll be glad to give out a commission for more heads: if this law hold in Vienna ten year, I'll rent the fairest house in it after three pence a bay. If you live to see this come to pass, say Pompey told you so.
>
> (235–40)

But comedy, concerned with communal continuance and therefore with social order, necessarily is concerned with the containing of sexual impulse within social order. Addressed is our need not just to continue, but to continue as civilized human beings. That is why the setting must be a city and why we are prepared to disengage from Pompey. The function of Froth, the heir of four-score pounds a year since his father died All-hallond eve, is not just as Pompey's straight man but as another butt; he is the mark, warned with judicial wit to avoid the acquaintance of "tapsters": "they will draw you, Master Froth, and you will hang them" (200–4). We are thus distinct from Pompey's customers. We root for the rogue and take delight in his escape by his wits—until the subject again becomes Claudio's impending execution and we realize that the scene has demonstrated Escalus's dictum, "Some run from brakes of ice [or is it "vice" that Shakespeare wrote] and answer none / And some condemned for a fault alone." But the moment of truth for Pompey comes earlier.

> *Esc.* Troth, and your bum is the greatest thing about you; so that, in the beastliest sense, you are Pompey the Great. Pompey, you are partly a bawd, Pompey, howsoever you colour it in being a tapster; are you not? Come, tell me true, it shall be the better for you.
>
> *Pom.* Truly, sir, I am a poor fellow that would live.
>
> *Esc.* How would you live, Pompey? By being a bawd? What do you think of the trade, Pompey? Is it a lawful trade?
>
> *Pom.* If the law would allow it, sir.
>
> (214–24)

In getting off with a warning, Pompey does not make a fool of Escalus; he does make a mockery of the mercy in Escalus's admonishment. This point reaches forward in the play to Escalus's spluttering outrage at Mrs. Overdone later.

> *Enter [severally]* Escalus; Provost, *and [Officers with]* Mistress *Overdone.*
>
> *Esc.* Go, away with her to prison.
>
> *Mis. O.* Good my lord, be good to me. Your honour is accounted a merciful man. Good my lord.
>
> *Esc.* Double and treble admonition, and still forfeit in the same kind! This would make mercy swear and play the tyrant.
>
> (III.ii.184–88)

The personifications are from traditions associated with the drama. Mercy always shows itself to be such in action whatever errancy it confronts. But confronted with Overdone (who newly earns her name in the play), Mercy itself would abandon its role to perform the diametrically opposite stock part, the tyrant. Pompey is going to do as he has done, live by being a bawd. He thanks Escalus for his good counsel, but tells us that he is going to "follow it as the flesh and fortune shall better determine" by continuing in his trade (249–53). Mercy to him proves itself a bawd. Here, in fact, is the first literal enactment (apart from the wise burgher's intervention on behalf of the houses of the city) of the idea only later verbally articulated at its climactic—but not last—literal enactment in the play: Claudio's begging his sister to yield to Angelo to save his life. Pompey analogically anticipates that poor fellow who would live by being a bawd.

It has not been observed that this idea, of mercy as a bawd, is a commonplace in Elizabethan discussions of the repentance of those, told "go and sin no more," who are going to repeat their sin. Shakespeare already had played on the idea in *Richard II*— and with clear allusion to God's relation to repentant sinful man— when King Henry would pardon Aumerle although York, protesting, furiously insists that "Fear, and not love, begets [his son's] penitence" (V.iii.56).

> Thy overflow of good converts to bad,
> And thy abundant goodness shall excuse
> This deadly blot in thy digressing son.
> *York.* So shall my virtue be his vice's bawd, . . .
>
> (64–67)

It is elsewhere in the drama of the time too. With characteristically impacted expression Tourneur sardonically invokes this same nexus of sense about the world of *The Revenger's Tragedy* (1606): "Save Grace the bawd, I seldom hear grace nam'd!" (I.iii.16)[44] Shakespeare's bawd is very calculatedly called "Madame Mitigation." The idea is, quite simply, fundamental to the actions, now to be played out, that make the very core of *Measure for Measure*. A pointer to that fact, as to the dilemma of the earthly prince wanting to be merciful, is supplied by the conclusion of this scene, which shows Escalus grieving at Claudio's fate and unable to see anything to be done about it. But to see that passage aright we must first consider the *dramatis persona* to whom Escalus speaks.

Escalus addresses a character Lever finds problematic, the Justice in the scene's entry: "*Enter Angelo, Escalus, and seruants,*

Iustice" (TLN 450). Bawcutt thinks this looks an afterthought, to provide Escalus with an interlocutor. That could be, but Shakespeare could hardly have been unaware that adding the character at *the start* of the scene was a major decision. Criticism often fails properly to register the force of silent actors, but the prolonged close presence of such a mute figure necessarily becomes insistent and demands imaginative entertainment. Shakespeare does not leave a character so pertinently identifiable by costume onstage for 237 lines before he speaks without a better reason than to be present at its end to tell Escalus the time or thank him for being asked to dinner (272–76). A robed justice stands by mute while Escalus presides over that judicial hearing. Lever finds the ten words he speaks in the last grouping "trivial"; but they include a crucial judgment, and it concerns Angelo's. It sets up the other position to debate the one Escalus, fortified by proverbial wisdom, takes, that ironically comments on his own mercy to Pompey.

> *Esc.*   It grieves me for the death of Claudio,
> But there's no remedy.
>
> *Justice.*   Lord Angelo is severe.
>
> *Esc.*   It is but needful.
> Mercy is not itself, that oft looks so;
> Pardon is still the nurse of second woe.
> But yet, poor Claudio! There is no remedy.
> Come, sir.
>
> > *Exeunt.*
> > (II.i.277–83)

The word *remedy* so deliberately repeated here is one that had been charged by its usage in the context of the Redemption, and it is to be used with that force by Isabella in her great speech on the ideal pattern of the judge, "He, which is the top of judgement," who "Found out the remedy" when "all the souls that were, were forfeit" (II.ii.73–76). In ironic contrast in the ensuing action are the remedies that are in fact proposed.

*   *   *

The lowlife characters and issues in this preceding scene insure that inquiry after the truth descends to a depth of quotidian experience: murky with the motions of appetite, dense with a particularity opportune for amoral artful dodging, and challenging to our capacity to name things aright. Thrown into sharp contrast in the high-minded debate to follow are not only the serious characters, the man of stricture in his judge's robes and the near-novice in her religious garb, but the theoretic cast of the debate between these committed idealists. They never even refer to the circumstances of Claudio's offense. They would argue the matter entirely with reference to opposed principles—a fact that gives their argument a more generalized power. It also assures them a basic sympathy in discourse as does, from the first, their shared detestation (and fear) of an offense involving a crucial part of human life in which neither is experienced. These characters have been set up; they surely will have to learn what other wretches feel.

The principles are justice and mercy, and the debate of these advocates and would-be embodiments reaches back in dramatic and cultural history to the Debate over man's fallen state by the Daughters of God before His throne. In that action, these contradictory attributes of God are met together and embrace in the mercy and justice of the Redemption. But what imitation of that action is possible below, in the world, and by vividly individual human beings who are as "man, proud man" is in Isabella's inspired delineation, "most ignorant of what he's most assur'd—His glassy essence" (118–21)—the image of God in his nature? This profound, and potentially deeply ironic, concern in this crucial scene and beyond has a neglected point of genesis early in this period of Shakespeare's own work. Though the circumstances are very different, the Prayer Scene in *Hamlet* also is sharply concerned with the ironies of delimited man's reach toward possession of the absolute mercy and justice mysteriously harmonized in the divine nature he is supposed to imitate. Shakespeare's interest in the power of this matter to define the paradox of man's place now is pursued through a unique vein of serious comic irony.

* * *

Shakespeare opens the scene with a fresh *dramatis persona* to bear the urgent hope that Angelo will relent about Claudio, choosing one not compromised, as Pompey is, in objecting to the sentence decreed through the awakened law, and distinguished from Escalus in not sharing his belief that Angelo's severity "is needful." He reintroduces a key minor character, the Provost who had explained to Claudio that in showing him to the world he acted not in evil disposition but "at Lord Angelo's special charge." The Provost, or (apparently) governor of the prison, is both experienced and humane, and in his view (as in ours) Claudio's sentence is flabbergasting.

> *Enter* Provost [*and a*] *Servant.*
>
> Servant. He's hearing of a cause: he will come straight; I'll tell him
> of you.
>
> Prov. Pray you, do. [*Exit Servant.*]
> I'll know
> His pleasure, may be he will relent. Alas,
> He hath but as offended in a dream;
> All sects, all ages smack of this vice, and he
> To die for't!
>
> (II.ii.1–6)

The scene indicatively starts, then, with revolt against Angelo's judgment, an insubordination that focuses on his will: "Is it your will that Claudio shall die tomorrow?" (7). The firm Angelo is offended. The Provost must himself crave pardon and ask what Angelo's will now shall be in the matter of Juliet, whose delivery approaches. Angelo's order for her speedy removal to a fitter place is interrupted by the Servant's announcing that "the sister of the man condemn'd / Desires access to" him. Thus the playwright arranges that the Provost's description of the sister Angelo has ordered be admitted—"a very virtuous maid; / And to be shortly of a sisterhood, / If not already"—is emphatically juxtaposed with his strict order for "the fornicatress [to] be remov'd" and strictly "needful . . . means for her provided" (18–25). This is the cue for Lucio's entrance with Isabella.

> *Enter* Lucio *and* Isabella.
>
> Prov. Save your honour! [*Going.*]
>
> Ang. Stay a little while.
> [*To Isabella*] Y'are welcome: what's your will?
>
> Isab. I am a woeful suitor to your honour;
> Please but your honour hear me.
>
> Ang. Well: what's your
> suit?

Isab.   There is a vice that most I do abhor,
           And most desire should meet the blow of justice;
           For which I would not plead, but that I must;
           For which I must not plead, but that I am
           At war 'twixt will and will not.

                                                        (25–33)

Why does Angelo tell the Provost, already going off, to "Stay a little while"? Lever says he is "kept back to witness the interview." That is the fact, and Shakespeare will show *his* reason for the witness: to have the Provost, in asides, reach beyond the deputy's authority to pray that heaven give Isabella moving graces to win Angelo, while Lucio is contrastingly present to urge her in a very different key to press her suit more warmly as woman to man. But we are not told *Angelo*'s reason, being left to surmise from context that he has a scruple about being by himself with her even though she is accompanied (and for the audience how accompanied!). The context immediately affords an answering scruple. The hesitant and diffident speech he gets from the very virtuous maid does not, as he asked, tell of her suit but rather of her scruples in bringing it; she ruminates a deeper answer to his initial "What's your will?" With Angelo's ugly word *fornicatress* still ringing in our heads as well as his question, her opening line must seem particularly oblique and self-preoccupied. Her maidenly evasion in referring indefinitely to the vice her hearers must identify is betrayed by the uncompromising verb she uses to express her aversion. Paronomasia on *whore/abhor,* perhaps irresistible, occurs even in the official Homily on Adultery, and Shakespeare uses it in *Othello,* the other play he wrote at this time.[45] But "Abhor that which is evil" (Rom. 12:9) is St. Paul's exhortation to the Christian; and Isabella's declaration "I am / At war 'twixt will and will not" reverberates with the Apostle's description of himself as carnal and captive despite knowledge that the law is spiritual.

> For I alowe not that which I do: for what I wolde, that I do not: but what I hate, that do I. . . . For I knowe, that in me, that is, in my flesh, dwelleth no good thing: for to wil is present with me: I finde no meanes to performe that which is good.
> For I do not the good thing, which I wolde, but the euil, which I wolde not, that do I. . . . I finde then by the Law, that when I wolde do good, euil is present with me.

For I delite in the Law of God, concerning the inner man:
But I se another law in my membres, rebelling against the law of my minde, & leading me captiue vnto the law of sinne, which is in my membres.

(Rom. 7:15; 18–19; 21–23)[46]

Dramatically, Isabella's scruple, which subtly melds with Angelo's, serves to articulate the awkward principle-challenging situation in which she finds herself with him. Her conflicted concern is that to plead for the offender, as she must, is to plead for a vice, the very carnality that she (like Angelo) does "most desire should meet the blow of justice."

Isabella's speech notably introduces a verbal practice crucial to the scene. Never in fact does she or Angelo precisely name Claudio's crime; it is "his fault," "this offence," "that evil . . . that did th' edict infringe," his "deed"; he "slipp'd" and is to answer "one foul wrong." This obtrusive suppression, so apt to these strictured characters, discloses—as Shakespeare mines it—a bonanza of dramatic expression. The effects are dual yet finally cohere. On the one hand, the brother's offense becomes general enough to reflect offending man's. That underscores Angelo's God-like role, empowering the contrasts of earthly with divine authority and the challenge to Angelo to show his newmade creation in God's image by imitating the mercy he, judged as he is, needs from Him "which is the top of judgment." But what "as you are" finally is pushed to mean is what Angelo's heart knows "That's like my brother's fault": "A natural guiltiness such as his is" (137–40). "My brother's fault" is the mark of everyman's fallen nature. The disobedience of man's flesh against his authority—what Lucio will not succeed in trivializing as "the rebellion of a codpiece" (III.ii.110–11)—as Augustine had famously explained, was the punishment for Adam and Eve's disobedience to God that made them ashamed of their nakedness.[47] That is written in our nature, as Angelo is invited to discover by asking what his heart must confirm of it.

On the other hand, the audience knows Claudio's offense, so the constantly evasive references, like all euphemism that in failing shouts the unspeakable thing it would hide, induces a growing consciousness of sexual frailty through the scene. There are readers who find impressive Angelo's sternly cogent defense of the deterrent law and of justice in enforcing it. They reckon so without the context that insists on the contentiousness of his "assumption that the exercise of law and the exercise of justice are the same,"[48] the inequity of his rigor, and his personal stake in it, by keeping before our minds the brother's actual offense. In this light, Angelo's sentence as solution to the problem of recidivism in this offender's rightly "answering one foul wrong," is as fantastic as it would be efficacious ("he lives not to act another" [104–5]). The audience's induced readiness to be aware of sexual frailty informs Isabella's taking the argument to the deputy's person and charges its sense of what Angelo is being forced to consider in himself. In this way Angelo can remain guarded throughout and they need not (and certainly ought not) ever touch, and the surprise of his soliloquy is as perfectly preserved as it is prepared.

Isabella's speech about her scruples in pleading the case establishes the logic of the interview's development. Her conflict leads her first to plead that the offense be condemned and the offender spared. When that fails, she abandons her brother to the past tense, declares the law just but severe, and offers to leave. Only Lucio's intervention stops her from so giving over the case, though his attempt to direct the performance of her role serves but to sharpen our apprehension of her character: "Kneel down before him, hang on his gown; / You are too cold" (44–45). But that is not Isabella's style; and to his criticism of her coldness and tameness of tongue she responds in her own way. The logic of her situation, as she herself has defined it, requires that she now plead for the offense as pardonable. The only way to convince the severe judge is to argue it lies in his power—and in the appropriate exercise of that power—to pardon the offender, to question therefore his imitation of true Authority in denying mercy, and to make him see the human weakness he shares with the condemned prisoner. He must see at last that he is a captive too and to the larger law that Vienna's awakened decree reflects. She questions the necessity of her brother's death, shows that the severe sentence issues from the judge's will, argues that his will would alter if he felt the "remorse"—the compassion, the fellow human feeling—she says she feels, and argues that his will could alter if he remembered mercy to be the most becoming attribute of greatness. A climax comes when she provokes him to imagine his and Claudio's situations reversed.

If he had been as you, and you as he,
You would have slipp'd like him, but he like you
Would not have been so stern.

Ang.   Pray you be gone.

Isab.   I would to heaven I had your potency,
         And you were Isabel! Should it then be thus?
         No; I would tell what 'twere to be a judge,
         And what a prisoner.

Lucio.   [to Isab.]   Ay, touch him: there's the vein.

                                                        (64–70)

Shakespeare punctuates this scene with arrested "goings," starting with the Provost. Having established with Isabella's offered exit this method of marking phases of the scene, he plays a variation in having a character invited to leave who doesn't. Angelo's dismissive rebuff to her effort to make him personally see both his potential weakness and his isolation in his severity finally strikes fire from her. By "potency" she means the power of his authority. But this is a woman talking to a man—the woman as powerless to the empowered man, with the boldness of lunging resentment at the fact. She injects herself into the question of exchanged places, imposed roles. Because this is so strongly personal ("And you were Isabel"), her wish quite different from the hypothetical exchange she proposed he consider just previously, it is implicitly her role as frustrated suitor that would be thrust on him. Of course she means to say she would tell how a judge should mercifully treat a prisoner. But the thing has been contrived so the concluding roles suggested are heard twisted in the wake of the earlier exchange so passionately proposed. Because her brother does not specifically come into it any more than her role should in imagination have been thrust on Angelo, the vehement rhetoric aimed at him makes us brush with the sense that she can herself tell what it is to be a prisoner and would tell what 'twere to be a merciful judge to him as prisoner. Lucio therefore properly completes the blank verse of her concluding line with its oddly surprising *prisoner*. From him, "Ay, touch him" has a physical cast, superimposed on the poetic drama's concern with "touching" Angelo's "mettle," and borne out by his wordplay that follows. I think Lever right to suppose *vein* figurative from the action of a physician to get at a patient's blood. That metaphor is reawakened to invigorate the obvious sense: "that's the right style of speech," "there's the way!"

But her next speech (73–79)—the great one beginning "Alas, alas! / Why, all the souls that were, were forfeit once"—must be in a differently personal vein, of exquisite Christian pity for his inability to see beyond the law, and then earnest urging of his need to see himself as he really is, exposed to God's judgment: a perspective that would lead him to be in utterance and action as man new made in the merciful Judge's image. The speech often is treated in discussion of Isabella or of the pertinent doctrine in the Sermon on the Mount. But its dramatic effect is in the clash so confidently expressed by Angelo before, to evince it, and after, to show he is yet untouched. The dialogue brings front stage that this is a scene where the characters are talking from contradictory premises. Shakespeare is sharply exploiting, not offering to settle, a large underlying problem from the world. Isabella's appeal to the individual begs a question. The claims on the magistrate—who is not supposed to bear the sword in vain (Rom. 13:4)—are different from those on the individual Christian. Regarding the law as an abstract entity and Isabella's brother a forfeit of it, Angelo makes clear he is as untouched by her noble speech as he was when he brushed aside her confrontational words as wasted ones.

> *Ang.*   Be you content, fair maid;
>   It is the law, not I, condemn your brother,
>   Were he my kinsman, brother, or my son,
>   It should be thus with him. He must die tomorrow.
>   (79–82)

We believe him, and were it not for the nature of the cause, we must see that impartiality as noble too.

But Angelo's emphasis on the impersonality of the law hides from him how personal his application of it is. We are used to regard the vagaries of subject-verb agreement in Shakespeare's Elizabethan English as substylistic. In "It is the law, not I, condemn your brother" it is not unexpressive that the verb's form is first person by attraction to the pronoun. The Duke never told Angelo to enforce the law in such "heavy sense" of it. It is the course that seemed good to his soul. That his position is extreme Isabella brings home to him by a surprising move. Her interest in Angelo's soul is displaced by her piercing concern for her brother's when she hears he is to die tomorrow—a most forceful way of introducing through the right consciousness the question of Claudio's preparation for death. She seems in crying "Spare him, spare him!" to be pleading for a stay of execution to prepare him for death when suddenly she switches focus to the uniqueness of the sentence.

Isab. Tomorrow? O, that's sudden.
Spare him, spare him!
He's not prepar'd for death. Even for our kitchens
We kill the fowl of season: shall we serve heaven
With less respect than we do minister
To our gross selves? Good, good my lord, bethink you:
Who is it that hath died for this offence?
There's many have committed it.

Lucio. [*to Isab.*] Ay, well said.
(83–90)

So now Angelo holds forth on the deterrent power of the awakened law and the pity shown by justice in its pitiless execution of the offender—only to be cut down by her going straight for the essential fact of the matter and its tyranny. Because in pursuing her point by searchingly developing the idea of imitation of the divine—already powerfully introduced—she climactically calls to account all deputy authority on earth.

Isab. Yet show some pity.
Ang. I show it most of all when I show justice;
For then I pity those I do not know,
Which a dismiss'd offence would after gall,
And do him right that, answering one foul wrong,
Lives not to act another. Be satisfied;
Your brother dies tomorrow; be content.
Isab. So you must be the first that gives this sentence,
And he, that suffers. O, it is excellent
To have a giant's strength, but it is tyrannous
To use it like a giant.
Lucio. [*to Isab.*] That's well said.
Isab. Could great men thunder
As Jove himself does, Jove would ne'er be quiet,
For every pelting petty officer

> Would use his heaven for thunder; nothing but thunder.
> Merciful heaven,
> Thou rather with thy sharp and sulphurous bolt
> Splits the unwedgeable and gnarled oak,
> Than the soft myrtle. But man, proud man,
> Dress'd in a little brief authority,
> Most ignorant of what he's most assur'd—
> His glassy essence—like an angry ape
> Plays such fantastic tricks before high heaven
> As makes the angels weep; who, with our spleens,
> Would all themselves laugh mortal.
>
> (100–24)

Any reader of Elizabethan writings on justice must come away impressed by the heavy emphasis on retributive justice. In that context, Isabella looks through Angelo to expose as Titan-like the presumptuous imaging of the divine by proud man in authority. The giant who would tyrannously use his strength "like a giant," would, could he thunder like Jove, "use his heaven for thunder, nothing but thunder." "Merciful heaven" is set off, with the effect of apostrophe, from the blank verse pattern in emphatic contrast. As Lever notes, the contrast of oak (or cedar) "struck by thunder while the pliant shrub survived was a commonplace for divine or royal justice and mercy"; but here the merciful restraint to hurl retributive bolts only at hardened and inveterate evil[49] notably is reserved to heaven alone. The likeness of divinity in his nature of which "proud man, / Dress'd in a little brief authority" is so assured is only "His glassy essence"—the fragile mirroring of the divine nature in his intellectual soul, of which he is "most ignorant." The true likeness of human authority in action is a lower mimic on the scale of being quite lacking man's "glassy essence": an angry ape performing his fantastic tricks on the stage of the world "before high heaven." Indignantly resentful disappointment charges this stunning indictment, a bitterly aggrieved chagrin at the humiliating absurdity of a vain playing of abominable man truly worthy of tears.

Angelo's silence, which Lucio and the Provost fill with excited hope of his yielding, Isabella takes as cue to draw her antagonist to open himself to her ultimate thrust. "We cannot weigh our brother with ourself" (127) invites curiosity by seeming to upend a core point in her argument. Her sayings instance worldly license

to superiors to do and say what would be regarded by their right
names, as profanation and blasphemy, in their inferiors. But that
relativism is here; it is not so above. Angelo with some irritation
bites.

Ang.   Why do you put these sayings upon me?

Isab.   Because authority, though it err like others,
Hath yet a kind of medicine in itself
That skins the vice o'th'top. Go to your bosom,
Knock there, and ask your heart what it doth know
That's like my brother's fault. If it confess
A natural guiltiness, such as is his,
Let it not sound a thought upon your tongue
Against my brother's life.

Ang.   [*aside*]   She speaks, and 'tis such sense
That my sense breeds with it.—Fare you well. [*Going.*]
                                                                     (134–43)

Angelo's aside is important—here is our first look behind the
facade at how he has been affected; but it is important too as an
example of how apt we are to misread through anticipation. Children hearing a story whose ending they know show more forbear-
ance in playing the game than many of Shakespeare's critics and,
as Sheridan wittily says, "those damned editors never can keep a
secret!" Johnson read "that my sense breeds with it" to mean simply "New thoughts are stirring in my mind, new conceptions are
hatched in my imagination." It was left to Capell (1780) to find
sensuality in "my sense" and to Ritson (1783) rhetorically to ratify
it: "Does not the deputy plainly mean, that *her wisdom* has raised
his desires?"[50] In Empson's elaborate study of the wordplay on
sense, the meaning sensuality "pokes its way forward and is gratified by the second use of the word as a pun."[51] But that is a judgment from the timeless world of contemplation. The drama is not
a timeless world, and that reading of *my sense,* though there is that
in the context to make it actively possible, remains a potentiality
awaiting realization. That comes in fact a full nineteen lines later;
and *sense* plainly has the proposed meaning during his soliloquy,
seven lines after that. Empson does not distinguish between what,
in consideration of what follows, the character must mean (and in
hindsight does) and the meaning an audience can here be *sure* of.
By telling us what is going on in Angelo, such readers displace

what is going on in the play, and destroy its suspense. In fact the character ends the line with "Fare you well" and ambiguously, unreadably, begins leaving.

That is the start of the climactic variation on the "going" routine. Isabella urgently calls "Gentle my Lord, turn back." He does, and tightly yields what is tantamount to a reprieve for Claudio: "I will bethink me. Come again tomorrow." And again he leaves, again to be turned back, this time by her offer of a bribe for that remarkable opportunity for the actor, "How! Bribe me?" With her clarification of her intent and its aftermath, everyone else departs and Angelo will be left onstage in the situation he had tried to put behind him—"that way going to temptation / Where prayer's cross'd."

> *Ang.*   I will bethink me. Come again tomorrow. [*Going.*]
>
> *Isab.*   Hark, how I'll bribe you: good my lord, turn back.
>
> *Ang.*   How! Bribe me?
>
> *Isab.*   Ay, with such gifts that heaven shall share with you.
>
> *Lucio.* [*to Isab.*] You had marr'd all else.
>
> *Isab.*   Not with fond sicles of the tested gold,
>   Or stones, whose rate are either rich or poor
>   As fancy values them: but with true prayers,
>   That shall be up at heaven and enter there
>   Ere sunrise: prayers from preserved souls,
>   From fasting maids, whose minds are dedicate
>   To nothing temporal.
>
> *Ang.*   Well: come to me tomorrow.
>   (144–56)

What comes across most clearly is her radiant beauty in her idealized commitment. There are flickers of a daringly devious underplay of unintended "sense" in "sickels" with "tested" followed by "stones," in "fancy," "be up" and "enter there." But of course the speech should be said in the joyous rapture of a paean to the value of the conventual life, as she imagines it. That is not as the Elizabethans imagined it, and the doctrine here is, for the audience intended, blatantly presumptuous and "fleshly." In her access of zeal she is presumptuous even in our superficial understanding. She has not yet taken her vows and already is directing the convent's battery of devoted souls in petitionary broadsides at full elevation. As Gless observes, the sex-preoccupied, manmade rules Francisca timorously cites show the nuns are indeed dedicated to something temporal.[52] Isabella's very argument puts their prayers on the same level as the folly-valued gold and stones with which they are contrasted—fancied religious payola with guaranteed direct transmission to the heavenly receiver. It *is* a bribe she offers. Angelo's tautly masked response to this enthusiasm is anticlimactic and deflative. But prayer continues as the motif structuring the beautifully managed lingering exit before Angelo finally is left alone.

> *Lucio.* [*to Isab.*] Go to: 'tis well; away.
>
> *Isab.*　Heaven keep your honour safe.
>
> *Ang.*　[*aside*]　　　　　　　　Amen.
> For I am that way going to temptation,
> Where prayer's cross'd.
>
> *Isab.*　　　　　　　　　At what hour tomorrow
> Shall I attend your lordship?
>
> *Ang.*　　　　　　　　　At any time 'fore noon.
>
> *Isab.*　Save your honour.　　　[*Exeunt all but Angelo.*]
>
> *Ang.*　　　　　　From thee: even from thy virtue!
>
> 　　　　　　　　　　　　　　　　(157–62)

Isabella's farewells at beginning and end, invoking God's protection of Angelo, inject the idea of Providence to set against the temptation confessed in his aside and later in his soliloquy. In the first he joins her prayer with rueful irony at his need of it that way he is going. Meanwhile she is going too, with the antsy Lucio ahead of her. But at the door she reverses for the momentary excruciation of arranging the time she will attend him tomorrow. This time his response to her farewell prayer, as he looks at where she has just stood, is not an amen but an ironic completion, in a cold sweat, identifying herself, indeed her virtue, as what he needs to be saved from.

His honestly questioning whether he has got that quite right makes the soliloquy memorable, and his appalled unfolding of the truth makes it compelling. Tonally the speech is varied and shifting, wonderfully articulating the disorder and alarm animating his rigid nature as he reacts to his own thoughts. The speech progresses through alternations of literal and figurative expression to accommodate the fresh discoveries of his breeding sense. But the progress itself is guaranteed by another iterated alternation, between attempts to evade or share responsibility for what he feels and dead-on acknowledgements that the evil he discovers is his. At the first he is almost drawn into such an evasion.

> What's this? What's this? Is this her fault, or mine?
> The tempter, or the tempted, who sins most, ha?
>
> (163–64)

But what follows are the definitively phrased absolute monosyllables that open out into the contrasted similes for doing under the sun that manifest his own corrupting use of "virtuous season." The casuistic question has been a dodge.

> Not she; nor doth she tempt; but it is I
> That, lying by the violet in the sun,
> Do as the carrion does, not as the flower,
> Corrupt with virtuous season.
>
> (165–68)

Incredulous, he asks if it can be that modesty in woman rather than "lightness" can more betray what he shares with other men—our "sense." Indignant, he rhetorically questions the course proposed if that were true—as though he were vividly preaching against it, showing what it profoundly means in terms drawn from property and building. Having what is common to the use, shall we prefer filthily to defile the temple of God devoted to His presence (see I Cor. 2:16–17), raze the sanctuary to build our privies there? The revulsion converts to self-disgust in the very act of discovering himself in the paradox of his desire.

> Having waste ground enough,
> Shall we desire to raze the sanctuary
> And pitch our evils there? O fie, fie, fie!
> What dost thou, or what art thou, Angelo?
> Dost thou desire her foully for those things
> That make her good? O, let her brother live!
> Thieves for their robbery have authority,
> When judges steal themselves. What, do I love her,
> That I desire to hear her speak again?

And feast upon her eyes? What is't I dream on?
O cunning enemy, that, to catch a saint,
With saints dost bait thy hook? Most dangerous
Is that temptation that doth goad us on
To sin in loving virtue.

(170–83)

Why does he refer to thieves? Because he wants her in the worst way: he desires her foully. That makes what follows, in a delicate tone remarkably shifted from the sardonic, disturbingly haunting because the very perversity of his desire is communicated by that use of "love." There is the pathos of a blind deprivation to put beside his shock at what he dreams of. That now precipitates the conclusion that "the cunning enemy" has caught him with the saintly bait used to catch saints. He has precedent for this comforting idea, but this temptation is not the devil's; the temptation that does the goading to sin alone suggests otherwise. His apostrophe to the "common enemy" is self-flattering religiosity, this time of the tempted. A more clearsighted formulation brings him to the climax of his understanding: that there can be dangerous temptation, goading us to sin, even in loving virtue. Though sin and grace, as virtue and vice, are contraries, though he may confidently refer to absolutes, no playwright could be more interested than Shakespeare—and in this play—in the evil aspect of things good and also the good that may be involved with things evil. In *Measure for Measure* the yarn of our experience is much more than mingled. Angelo's insight into the general paradox revealed in his situation crystallizes our realization that it is this indicative idea—of the capacity for sin in the love of virtue—that has been literally enacted. Isabella's more complex enactment of it is to come.

The other thing that needs saying about this closing of the scene is that it is a cliff-hanger. It does not end "tragically" with commitment to a plan of evil action, though all the matter to imagine one is to hand in his lust, his office, her offer of a bribe, in the expectations of the "monstrous ransom" story itself. Instead we have a self-ignorant character's eye-opened musing on others' susceptibility to sexual infatuation that used to evince from him only contemptuous superiority and puzzlement.

Never could the strumpet
With all her double vigour, art and nature,

> Once stir my temper: but this virtuous maid
> Subdues me quite. Ever till now
> When men were fond, I smil'd, and wonder'd how. *Exit.*

(183–87)

He confesses himself subdued by "this virtuous maid"; but it is not certain what, after this very moral self-recognition, he is going to do about it. That withholding does not exist just to heighten attention to his soliloquy that will open the scene of their scheduled interview to come. It is strategic, for the evil deeds this temptation leads Angelo into will never be permitted to have the actual consequence he intends. They are to be forestalled and transmuted, and the character that story leads us to expect should be the one to accomplish this is the very one who next appears on stage.

That that is the case gives special force to the reintroduction of the Duke in his friar disguise, for it now would appear that we have the authority of church and state to set against the consequence of Angelo's temptation. But the Duke, who has lent the power entrusted to him to another, by his own admission had not succeeded in using it entirely aright; and the "Friar" (whom we might well expect to prove a meddler in worldly affairs) is a counterfeit. The scene's opening lines emphasize just that.

> *Enter [severally]* Duke *[disguised as a Friar]*
> *and* Provost.
>
> *Duke.*   Hail to you, Provost—so I think you are.
> *Prov.*   I am the Provost. What's your will, good Friar?

(II.iii.1–2)

Indeed, over two centuries of antifraternal writings and representation assure that the very part the Duke is counterfeiting itself could be expected to represent counterfeit religion. Shakespeare is not so crude of course, or so intolerant. The Duke has been instructed well how to "formally in person bear like a true Friar." Having learned at Juliet's entrance of Claudio's plight and hers, his catechizing to test her attitude toward her sin and the soundness of her repentance is properly searching and doctrinally flawless. We simply are made very conscious that this religious role is one he is playing, because the character opposite is proved by his enquiry to be the living embodiment of true religion. She interrupts his lengthy explanation of the attitude toward her sin and shame her repentance should *not* spring from; she already is where she should be to say the fifteen words that show her repentance sound.

> *Duke.*   Then was your sin of heavier kind than his.
>
> *Juliet.* I do confess it, and repent it, father.
>
> *Duke.*   'Tis meet so, daughter; but lest you do repent
>   As that the sin hath brought you to this shame,
>   Which sorrow is always toward ourselves, not heaven,
>   Showing we would not spare heaven as we love it,
>   But as we stand in fear—
>
> *Juliet.* I do repent me as it is an evil,
>   And take the shame with joy.
>
> (28–36)

Rosalind Miles has remarked the absence of the play element that usually attaches to the ruler-in-disguise motif.[53] A thought of Shakespeare's Rosalind (though hardly fair) will show how little fun for the Duke the liberation that might be expected of disguise produces. That the entertainment will largely be reserved for the audience is shown in his first tryout as Friar where Juliet appears to upstage the Duke because his performance serves as a foil to intensify what she is for real.

Juliet's entire role, apart from her mute appearances in I.ii and the finale, consists of the sixty-three words she speaks in this brief scene. But the utterance is irreducible and the consistency absolute: this is one of the most intensely beautiful small parts in Shakespeare. Her directness, her spare wholeness of response, the completeness of her attention, the purity of her tone—these tell the strength, intelligence, honesty, and clarity of the character's being. She is genuinely humble, truly patient in bearing her guilt and shame, and properly self-loving.

> *Duke.*   Love you the man that wrong'd you?
>
> *Juliet.* Yes, as I love the woman that wrong'd him.
>
> *Duke.*   So then it seems your most offenceful act
>   Was mutually committed?
>
> *Juliet.*   Mutually.
>
> (24–27)

How narrow, if pertinent, an inference he draws! The Duke-Friar
had announced himself "Bound by my charity, and my bless'd order, . . . come to visit the afflicted spirits / Here in the prison"
(3–5). Charity has a more arresting guise in Juliet's response. Here
human love and Christian charity are inseparable and acknowledgment of sin and forgiveness of her wronger indissolubly bound to
charity. In Shakespeare's searching irony, it is to the character
Angelo calls "the fornicatress," the one even the understanding
Provost says "hath blistered her report," that we must turn for the
play's most compelling representation of religion integrated in a
human life. Satisfied with her spiritual state, the Friar preparatively
announces he is "going with instruction" to her partner, who "as
I hear, must die tomorrow" (37–38), and exits to leave Juliet alone
with the Provost for a brief concluding grouping. Set against what
must seem the insensitive factuality of the Friar, they realize for
us the enormity of Claudio's pitiable death. The emotional climax
of Juliet's role is in her suffering consciousness of the meaning of
"must die tomorrow."

> Grace go with you: *Benedicite!*   *Exit.*
>
> *Juliet.* Must die to-morrow! O injurious love,
>   That respites me a life, whose very comfort
>   Is still a dying horror!
>
> *Prov.*   'Tis pity of him.   *Exeunt.*
>   (39–42)

Commentators have been notably unhappy in dealing with that
speech. It is very hard. The perception is paradoxical, the expression compacted, starting with oxymoron. The order is laid out in
nested relative clauses, but the referents are assumed, the thought
inclusively telescoped, merging past and future in the present of
her life. Since she comments from her situation, it is essential to
visualize it. The term of her pregnancy is almost full; the Provost
speaks to her of the arrangements for her delivery just before the
Friar's "Repent you, fair one, of the sin you carry?" (19) His primary reference is to the burden of her conscience. But, though
Hogan notes that "carry" does not appear with the meaning "to
be pregnant with" before 1776, it appears so here.[54] It is clear
by the juxtaposition that Shakespeare is anchoring the abstract
consideration of repentance in the concrete circumstance of her

visible pregnancy. The testing of her penitence has reference to it in "this shame" as evidence of her "most offenceful act." She now refers to the fact that she has been spared because of her pregnancy. Her complaint is against what she must apostrophize in oxymoron because it is the love that her being is about that is injurious. It "respites" her "a life"—a delay for a limited time in which to live—in impregnating her with the new life that testifies to the love condemning her partner to die. But the very comfort of that life—her being in love, her oneness with him in the child and her love—is by virtue of that identity the horror of his dying that does not die while she lives. The very coherence of her being makes her pain so complete in apprehending "must die tomorrow."

In contrast, the crosscut offers Angelo's weary contemplation of the disintegrated being revealed to him in his attempts to pray.

Ang. When I would pray and think, I think and pray
To several subjects: Heaven hath my empty words,
Whilst my invention, hearing not my tongue,
Anchors on Isabel: Heaven in my mouth,
As if I did but only chew his name,
And in my heart the strong and swelling evil
Of my conception.

(II.iv.1–7)[55]

He is bored with studying the state; the gravity he secretly takes pride in he finds nugatory. The evil of his "conception" moves him to acknowledge the irreducibility of the "blood" of human nature that makes the awesome outer appearance of "place" but the imposition of "false seeming." Evidently, what the blood would devilishly urge under the guise of such seeming prompts him cynically to propose designating diabolic identity the good angel that the tempter traditionally would appear to be.

Blood, thou art blood.
Let's write good angel on the devil's horn—
'Tis not the devil's crest.

(15–17)

"Good angel" is not properly "the devil's crest" (or cognizance denoting essential character); it better fits the hypocrisy of "place" as the "blood" that occupies it would use its power and seeming. His own name is just right for the part he implies he will play.

At a servant's imagination-inviting announcement that "one Isabel, a sister, desires access" to him (18), he describes how his blood musters to his heart, making it unable and unfitting his other parts, finally likening this distress to a disordered populace quitting their role in the body politic to offend "a well-wish'd king" with crowding to his presence (26–30). Here Shakespeare makes the point about the disorder of Angelo's single state of man, but dilutes the tragic concentration by alluding to King James's experience during his visit to the Exchange. In the dramatic context the placatively complimental allusion is a deliberate distraction.[56] The focus is not to be on the development of Angelo's disordered inner experience. The prey of this nervous tempter is the one we expect to prove most illuminated by the neglected little scene that Shakespeare placed with such calculation between the two interviews of precise deputy and devoted "sister." With Isabella's offer of a bribe Shakespeare had disengaged moral initiative from her and shifted it to the audience. The playwright then found in Juliet a remarkably economic way implicitly to prepare the audience to take the measure of Isabella's coherence.

Only its conclusion proved the first interview to have been a temptation. In this interview the audience expects one, and with the tables turned, the other of these paralleled repressed figures to be assayed. Audience interest is focused, and not without anticipatory amusement, by the prospect of the aroused but inexperienced Angelo's attempted seduction of the equally inexperienced, assertively bright and self-consciously virtuous "sister." That focus immediately is tightened when, faced with Angelo's conclusion that her brother "must die," she concerns herself with the urgency of preparing his soul for death rather than renewing her plea for his life. This initial movement recalls that the first interview ends with her offer to leave. But this time there is no Lucio insistently to prompt "Give't not o'er so." The hardly disinterested Angelo is obliged to set about cunningly reengaging her with the objective of saving her brother's life. The roles are reversed, and the action of the tempter urging mercy to save a brother replayed.

His first attempt is sly but usefully confused. He begins with the detestation of "these filthy vices" he knows she shares, but then startlingly equates the unpardonability of illicit coining of life through fornication with the theft of life by murder. That is bait dangled for the character who risked worldly relativism in questioning "Must he needs die?" "Who is it that hath died for this offence?"—and she bites, now seemingly assuming a God as indifferent to equity as Angelo.

> *Ang.* Ha? Fie, these filthy vices! It were as good
> To pardon him that hath from nature stolen
> A man already made, as to remit
> Their saucy sweetness that do coin heaven's image
> In stamps that are forbid. 'Tis all as easy
> Falsely to take away a life true made,
> As to put mettle in restrained means
> To make a false one.
>
> *Isab.* 'Tis set down so in heaven, but not in earth.
>
> *Ang.* Say you so? Then I shall pose you quickly.
> Which had you rather, that the most just law
> Now took your brother's life; or, to redeem him,
> Give up your body to such sweet uncleanness
> As she that he hath stain'd?
>
> (42–55)

But if her response, admitting a world where fornication is pardonable, gives him an opening for his proposal, his own self-consistency assures that his formulation of it will contradict that seductive drift. For the law under which her brother is to die can only be thought "most just" by reference to the absoluteness of God's under which fornication is as deadly a sin as murder. How is she to "redeem" her brother by giving up her body to such "sweet uncleanness" as Juliet whom her brother "stain'd" without committing her brother's offense?

> *Isab.*   Sir, believe this:
> I had rather give my body than my soul.
>
> *Ang.* I talk not of your soul: our compell'd sins
> Stand more for number than for accompt.
>
> *Isab.*   How say you?
>
> *Ang.* Nay, I'll not warrant that: for I can speak
> Against the thing I say.
>
> (55–60)

She is no more aware that she is being a tease here than she could have been conscious that she was the provocation of his temptation. She does not begin to imagine that his poser of a question is anything but hypothetical. Under the privilege of that assumption she in effect generalizes the hypothesis and evasively gives a trick answer suggesting she could regard her body and soul separately. He would not talk of her soul at all and suggests a context in which her hypothetical act would be pardonable, though now acknowledged a sin. But that requires introducing an idea skirted in his original proposal—compulsion. Why does he shrink back from warranting his assumption? The idea that "compelled sins are no sins" was proverbial (Tilley, S475). But serious writers on the question, such as those Gless cites,[57] claim only that such sins are more pardonable, depending on the degree of consent of the will involved; so Angelo (remembering his audience) backs away from the larger claim. That is useful to Shakespeare in relation to his audience. The popular idea about compelled sins sometimes is assumed in versions of the "monstrous ransom" story, and the dramatist plainly does not want it assumed here. That Angelo would have her commit a sin that could imperil her soul is not her hysterical defense, but intensely the fact of the matter. Critics who call his extortion "rape" actually blur Angelo's "most pernicious purpose," which is to win not merely her submission but her consent. He wants her to give him "love"; his demand finally will be "Fit thy consent to my sharp appetite" (143; 160). Angelo says "I talk not of your soul" and ends by focusing the context on exactly that.

His second try goes straight to the heart of the matter with a fine casuistical question that both recalls Juliet and also suggests that the travesty of the Redemption in his original proposal might not have been so dismissably outrageous as it seemed.

> Answer to this:
> I—now the voice of the recorded law—
> Pronounce a sentence on your brother's life:
> Might there not be a charity in sin
> To save this brother's life?
>
> (60–64)

But he neglects to make clear that the same proposal is still being hypothesized, thus producing the telling comic confusion of her offering at the peril of her soul to undertake his sin while having the wrong one in mind.

Isab.	Please you to do't.
	I'll take it as a peril to my soul;
	It is no sin at all, but charity.
Ang.	Pleas'd you to do't, at peril of your soul,
	Were equal poise of sin and charity.
Isab.	That I do beg his life, if it be sin,
	Heaven let me bear it; you granting of my suit,
	If that be sin, I'll make it my morn prayer
	To have it added to the faults of mine,
	And nothing of your answer.

(64–73)

Since the sin she has in mind—*his* saving of this brother—she is sure is charity, her offer to pray to bear the onus of it is as grandstandingly easy as her conventual assumption about souls with transferable charge accounts is mockable. That she is being set up in her self-approbation just as his frustration in getting her to follow his sexual drift (again to be registered by the pun on *sense*) forces him to "speak more gross" is made clear by their next exchange.

Ang.	Nay, but hear me;
	Your sense pursues not mine; either you are ignorant,
	Or seem so, crafty; and that's not good.
Isab.	Let me be ignorant, and in nothing good,
	But graciously to know I am no better.
Ang.	Thus wisdom wishes to appear most bright
	When it doth tax itself: as these black masks
	Proclaim an enciel'd beauty ten times louder
	Than beauty could, display'd.

(73–81)

Her complacent mock-modest claim to gracious wisdom in ignorance deserves his put-down and helps frame our attention to her long-awaited response as he now spells out her hypothetical dilemma to an either-or.

Ang.   Admit no other way to save his life—

. . . .

No earthly mean to save him, but that either
You must lay down the treasures of your body
To this suppos'd, or else to let him suffer:
What would you do?

Isab.   As much for my poor brother as myself;
That is, were I under the terms of death,
Th'impression of keen whips I'd wear as rubies,
And strip myself to death as to a bed
That longing have been sick for, ere I'd yield
My body up to shame.

Ang.   Then must your brother die.

Isab.   And 'twere the cheaper way.
Better it were a brother died at once,
Than that a sister, by redeeming him,
Should die for ever.

                                                  (88, 95–108)

A heroine in a melodrama might hold our thrilled sympathy by
honestly saying, "I would rather die than so yield my body even
though my brother perish." Shakespeare fascinates us with the
ironic self-exposure of an evasive self-deceiver whose first, circu-
itous answer avoids mentioning the consequence for her poor
brother. Her response, in emphasizing charity and shame at its
beginning and end, looks back to Juliet. It also prepares for her
scene with Claudio, for the question preoccupying her there will
be: will he do as much for her as she would have him do for herself?
Here (as Gless observes) she does not, as Juliet, say that she loves
her brother as herself, but rather that she would do as much for
him as for herself—were she under the terms of death. Her self-
regarding reformulation of the hypothesized dilemma permits her
rapturously to contemplate her own embrace of death while ignoring her brother's actual execution. Ironically, what makes her eager
fantasy of martyrdom pertinent is the powerful eroticism with
which it is charged. "Loving virtue" is given another sensational,
and sensual, twist. She exhibits a perversion of sexuality that is
the obverse of Angelo's and in this sublimated passion the ultimate
tease of his lust. Meanwhile, to the paradox of "charity in sin" she
has preferred that of uncharitableness in virtue. The abandonment
of charity immediately is followed by the abandonment of the Ex-

emplar of Mercy who "found out the remedy" so she need not "die forever." Her cost accounting of the alternatives is stacked by erroneous salvific doctrine; for her salvation does not depend upon her works.[58] She deploys a doctrine that says her frailty would be unforgivable in order to justify rejection of what *she* regards a fate worse than death.

That is not to say that her distinction between "lawful mercy" and "foul redemption," when challenged that she would be "as cruel as the sentence," is not warranted; only that there is irony for an audience that knows the Redemption involved "Ignomy in ransom" (109–13). In the discussion of frailty that follows, she is unguarded by any appeal to Christian charity, the mercy of a re-deeming God, or the imaging of God in man—the motif renewed early in this interview by Angelo's view of fornication as counter-feit coining of "heaven's image." That motif recurs here, ironically, only through her reference to the marring of creation in that image when men take advantage of the frailty of women, who she admits are "credulous to false prints."

Ang.   Nay, women are frail too.

Isab. Ay, as the glasses where they view themselves,
Which are as easy broke as they make forms.
Women?—Help, heaven! Men their creation mar
In profiting by them. Nay, call us ten times frail;
For we are soft as our complexions are,
And credulous to false prints.

Ang.   I think it well;
And from this testimony of your own sex—
Since I suppose we are made to be no stronger
Than faults may shake our frames—let me be bold.

                                                    (123–32)

Her admission he announces the cue for his bold invitation to her to be what she outwardly appears, to show herself a woman in being frail as she was made. Again her "sense" pursues not his—(for that, to be fair, is what is going to happen). She can scarcely believe it is not some other sort of trap he is laying for her even when he plainly declares himself in his desire. Only when he asks her to believe him on his honor that his words express his purpose, that he *is* what he appears, does her outrage denounce him as "Seeming, seeming!"—the very personification of false appearance.

> I will proclaim thee, Angelo, look for't.
> Sign me a present pardon for my brother.
> Or with an outstretch'd throat I'll tell the world aloud
> What man thou art.
>
> (149–53)

The honorable judge's outrage, earlier, at her offer to bribe him reverberates in the chaste sister's outcry at his extortionate demand of a bribe. But threatening to proclaim him, she attempts to extort from him a pardon for her brother, an action that ironically pronounces these antagonists to be counterparts, even "doubles."

Much of the brilliance of this remarkable scene is in the dramatic wit by which its shape and meaning are realized by reference to the first interview. There we follow a persuasion which, in reaching the ground for Christian mercy in the frailty of the judge, succeeds—as we later discover in soliloquy—only in facilitating the arousal of his lust for the intercessor, so that he is tempted to sin in loving virtue. She exposes the questionableness of the justice in his God-like rule, but her effort to convince him to be God-like in mercy evinces his carnality. In this scene, the corrupted judge suggests the religious intercessor be a redeemer, that she take on the circumstance of human flesh to assume the sins of others in order to save her brother from the all-binding law. Whether that is a spiritual opportunity, despite the intention of the proposer, depends on whether the charitable end truly may justify the sinful means consented to. But the possibility is enough for the charity and mercy of the intercessor to be challenged as was the justice of the Duke's substitute and God's.

However, this proposal certainly is a temptation, and the tempter's persuasion reaches the ground not of mercy but of carnal sin, exposing her share in the human frailty of her sex. But Isabella never would stoop (as she will say) "To such abhorr'd pollution." That precisely is why he lusts to compel her consent. And now that his mask is off, coldly confident his false outweighs her true and that his repute will make her threatened proclamation of him smell of calumny, he gives his sensual race the rein and inexorably tightens his grip by tyrannically threatening that her "unkindness" will assure a lingering death for her brother if she refuses to fit her consent to his sharp appetite. The matter is left unconcluded as in the first interview: "Answer me tomorrow" (166). But the argument from character coincides with the argument from design. She is no more to be pried from her refusal by this coercion than he was earlier persuaded to be merciful. The structural parallelism of the two interviews prepares us to expect that the temptation to which she is vulnerable is not the one he proposes but the one she will reveal in soliloquy concluding the scene. We are primed for the pleasure of a significantly fulfilled symmetry in which the soliloquy discloses a prepared surprise, that the persuasion to be merciful has evinced her carnality, her version of the dangerous temptation to sin in loving virtue. The radical variation is in her unconsciousness of the fact; the recognition is ours, and that is established at the start.

The speech begins, arialike, "To whom should I complain?" (170) One would have supposed a postulant in her religious costume would know the answer to that question. "God *is* our hope and strength, and helpe in troubles, readie to be found" (Ps. 46:1). You complain to One who knows and understands, who can be trusted, and relied on for help. Instead, Isabella considers the world she is part of. Angelo was right about his name, repute, and place—his accusation-overwhelming "honour." "Did I tell this, who would believe me?" (170–71) Apostrophizing "perilous mouths," she indicts the world only exemplified in Angelo, and does so in moral, not specifically religious, terms: a world of seeming, where the tongue of moral judgment, as equivocal as convenient, bids law bow to corrupted will, "Hooking both right and wrong to th'appetite, / To follow as it draws!" (171–76) Where to turn in such a world, whom to rely upon, but her brother! We readily see she is setting up a disappointment to come by relying, in order to preserve the honor of her body, on a being "fall'n by prompture of the blood." But the sister is more like the brother than she imagines.

> I'll to my brother.
> Though he hath fall'n by prompture of the blood,
> Yet hath he in him such a mind of honour,
> That had he twenty heads to tender down
> On twenty bloody blocks, he'd yield them up
> Before his sister should her body stoop

> To such abhorr'd pollution.
> Then, Isabel live chaste, and brother, die:
> More than our brother is our chastity.
> I'll tell him yet of Angelo's request,
> And fit his mind to death, for his soul's rest. *Exit.*
>
> (176–86)

She draws a conclusion from that trust in a close for the soliloquy carefully modulated by scene-ending couplets. These encapsulate her in the axiom for herself she settles on and render conventionally opaque her simple announcement of two elementary intentions for the promised scene with her brother. That modulation confirms the implicit evolution of irony from pathos in the whole speech. In pronouncing that comfortably self-justifying general dictum, she has a perilous mouth that bids the law make curtsy to her will and hooks right to the appetite. For charity, not chastity, fulfills the law. Her "honorable" solution is not for the honor of God; it is "fleshly," and though "virtuous," sprung of self-love. The "thing enskied and sainted" is very much a member of the world in which she moves.

* * *

The swift crosscut excites pleasurable anticipation by immediately contrasting the condemned Claudio's "hope of pardon from Lord Angelo" with Isabella's concluding intention to "fit his mind to death." A scene is required in which she will display the consequence of her temptation as this last one displayed that of Angelo's. But that the Duke-Friar, as prepared in the Juliet scene, is beforehand in effecting this role of spiritual guide to Claudio shifts the initiative away from her, and with it, as the Friar's speech assures, the focus claimed by the dominant character. It is a crucial speech, and we need to have it before us.

> *Enter* Duke [*disguised*] *and* Provost [*with*] Claudio.

> Duke. So then you hope of pardon from Lord Angelo?
>
> Cla.   The miserable have no other medicine
> But only hope:
> I have hope to live, and am prepar'd to die.
>
> Duke. Be absolute for death: either death or life

Shall thereby be the sweeter. Reason thus with life:
If I do lose thee, I do lose a thing
That none but fools would keep. A breath thou art,
Servile to all the skyey influences
That dost this habitation where thou keep'st
Hourly afflict. Merely, thou art Death's fool;
For him thou labour'st by thy flight to shun,
And yet run'st toward him still. Thou art not noble;
For all th'accommodations that thou bear'st
Are nurs'd by baseness. Thou'rt by no means valiant;
For thou dost fear the soft and tender fork
Of a poor worm. Thy best of rest is sleep;
And that thou oft provok'st, yet grossly fear'st
Thy death, which is no more. Thou art not thyself;
For thou exists on many a thousand grains
That issue out of dust. Happy thou art not;
For what thou hast not, still thou striv'st to get,
And what thou hast, forget'st. Thou art not certain;
For thy complexion shifts to strange effects
After the moon. If thou art rich, thou'rt poor;
For, like an ass whose back with ingots bows,
Thou bear'st thy heavy riches but a journey,
And Death unloads thee. Friend hast thou none;
For thine own bowels which do call thee sire,
The mere effusion of thy proper loins,
Do curse the gout, serpigo, and the rheum
For ending thee no sooner. Thou hast nor youth, nor age,
But as it were an after-dinner's sleep
Dreaming on both; for all thy blessed youth
Becomes as aged, and doth beg the alms
Of palsied eld: and when thou art old and rich,
Thou hast neither heat, affection, limb, nor beauty
To make thy riches pleasant. What's yet in this
That bears the name of life? Yet in this life
Lie hid moe thousand deaths; yet death we fear
That makes these odds all even.

(III.i.1–41)

The Duke's major speech in contempt of life certainly has got the critics' attention, but in all the arguing about it the point seems to get lost that *that* is its first function. The focus moves to the Duke *here*—at the start of the scene—not at the so-called split in the play later in it. The spotlight is intensified by the fact that his

performance as Friar here is startlingly different from that earlier
with Juliet. Shakespeare emphasized the difference in the present
context by giving to the Duke's interlocutor the specifically Christian terms and concepts that might have been expected from the
Friar who dealt with Juliet's sin and repentance with such
priestly exactitude.

> *Cla.*   I humbly thank you.
>   To sue to live, I find I seek to die,
>   And seeking death, find life. Let it come on.
>
>   (41–43)

Arthur Kirsch says that "unlike many critics of the play, Claudio
at least does not misunderstand" the Friar.[59] To the contrary, Claudio understands the context-invoked conventions of the spiritual
exercise from the Christian art of dying, and responds appropriately to that exercise. But his is so pat a formulation of the Christian paradox of living and dying that its coming after the specific
counsel he has heard makes his response seem neither deeply conceived nor felt. His "let it come on," after all, marks a resolution
we are anticipating will be assayed. It will be just ten lines until
Claudio will be seeking of his sister a very different "comfort" in
a very different tone (53). Now that is very human—and comic.
In fact we have in the apparent viewpoints of Friar and condemned
an amusing reversal of roles. The Friar's pseudo-Ciceronian "Reason thus with life," in arguing contempt of death through contempt
of life, puts down Claudio's "hope to live" without reference to
Christian doctrine, even leaving uncorrected his worlding's conception of "hope" as the only "medicine" of the miserable. It is
remarkable from a strictly Christian viewpoint not only for what
it omits but for what it includes, which reaches to "lawless and
incertain thought" (as well as a distortive use of Lucretius) as much
as Claudio's later version of the *contemplatio mortis* in his speech
on death. These speeches Lever justly sees as subtle distortions of
the two-part Christian exercise in preparation for death they recall.

This performance of the Duke as Friar is adjusted, not without
irony, to the person addressed, and to the situation as the Duke
perceives it. Kirsch says there is no need of any reference to Christ
or salvation because "the friar is the Duke, and I think we are
confident that . . . he has no intention of letting Claudio die." How

does the critic know that? Where has the Duke, or Shakespeare, tipped his hand in that regard? As suggested earlier, we might find a hint in his speech about decorum going "all athwart"; beheading those guilty of premarital intercourse seems much too draconian to sort with that view of his dukedom's disorder. And to this we might add the very promise generated by Shakespeare's merging in the Duke the authority appealed to in many versions of the "monstrous ransom" story with the ruler-in-disguise-amongst-his-subjects. But otherwise the Duke gives no indication whatever, from the point that he learns of Claudio's plight in the Juliet scene, that he means to save him. Kirsch has this thing the wrong way round. We may surmise the Duke is not going to let Claudio die because of the manner of his preparing him for death.

Leavis thinks that of all the attitudes toward death in this play so unusually preoccupied with it, the indifference to death displayed by the unfit-to-live-or-die Barnardine "comes nearest to that preached by the Friar"; and he claims that "the whole play" is an "implicit criticism" of the Friar's speech. Leavis never explains how that view is to be reconciled with his insistence—variously shared by many others—"that the Duke's attitude, nothing could be plainer, *is* meant to be ours—his total attitude, which is the total attitude of the play."[60] This speech, at the very point when the disguised Duke begins to intervene in the matter of Claudio, though it obviously cannot be taken to represent "his total attitude," initiates a rather more complex, and dissociated, relation of audience to Duke. The speech, which indulges the pleasure of a bemused disillusioned ironic consciousness, develops with greater sophistication and depth the kind of effect achieved by Jacques's speech on the Ages of Man. The satirically toned, one-sided emphasis in what purports to be a survey of our life, provokes objecting awareness of what the privileged bias omits or denies, but also acknowledgment of the experiential acuity of its partial truth. The crack about children—"thine own bowels" in biblical phrase, forsooth—is pure worldly cynicism; the fine lines on youth and age admired by Johnson and Eliot are all too telling. In the crucial put-down preceding the dispelling of such illusions as happiness, certainty of being, riches and friendship—"Thou art not thyself; / For thou exists on many a thousand grains / That issue out of dust"—Lever finds "pagan philosophy and Christian doctrine blended." But here it is just to say, as Paul Hammond observes of the speech as a whole, that it "goes further toward cynical disparagement of life than either a stoic philosopher or a Christian theologian would permit."[61] That the irony both in and of the outlook is located in the Duke's conscious adaptation of the spiritual exercise, relates to the kind of remedy that is going to be provided for imprisoned man condemned to death, just as the expansion of our consciousness (which restrictive Christian interpretation would collapse) surely relates to Shakespeare's bringing off the audacity of placing man in so profound a circumstance at the center of a "comedy."

The two big Angelo-Isabella scenes preceding, for all their power, eloquence, and arresting and varied emotion, are essentially ironic in structure and import. In each, both characters are probed, but one particularly makes a claim on the other to play a role, and that character is threatened, tempted, and exposed. In the Claudio-Isabella grouping that now ensues, after provision for the Friar's concealment during their dialogue, Shakespeare delights us by repeating this dramatic idea with two characters at the same time. Hazlitt wished Shakespeare "had provided a more disinterested trial for his heroine."[62] But that Isabella has an interest in her brother's dying, and is not at all sure that he is going to share that interest, is what makes the scene and its mutual deflations and exposures possible. Given the Duke-Friar's opening gambit, and our awareness that he is overhearing the interview, and that these characters therefore are not isolate and desolate in their interlocked failure of one another, the comically ironic potentialities of the situation are liberated to affect us at the same time as the excruciations of the characters in their melodrama make their claims to move us. That complexity is the central fact of their dialogue, and its means of discovering import, from first to last. The scene is a remarkable instance of that near-to-cruel streak that comedy shows when discomfiting characters whose "seeming" deserves exposure. What really limits the disengagement of the audience is not the fate of the characters, but the fate and experience of the audience, its vulnerability to the import. Claudio (for instance) speaks so eloquently not of what he fears of death but of what we do.

> The weariest and most loathed worldly life
> That age, ache, penury and imprisonment

Can lay on nature, is a paradise
To what we fear of death.

(128–31)

The first move of the dialogue affirms that the opening statement of the scene in the Friar's unorthodox speech was thematic. The terms and urgency of Claudio's queries—"what's the comfort? . . . Is there no remedy?" (53; 60)—ironically abort his recent claimed discovery about seeking death to find life. Isabella too moves from pretense, in her fantastic preparation for death which is as offbeat in its way as the Friar's, to a consideration of the issue between them in which the Christian viewpoint will be submerged.

Cla.   Now, sister, what's the comfort?

Isab.   Why,
As all comforts are: most good, most good indeed.
Lord Angelo, having affairs to heaven
Intends you for his swift ambassador,
Where you shall be an everlasting leiger.
Therefore your best appointment make with speed;
Tomorrow you set on.

Cla.   Is there no remedy?

Isab.   None, but such remedy as, to save a head,
To cleave a heart in twain.

(53–62)

Not her soul, but her heart. In her hearty-cheerful attempt to find most good comfort in Claudio's swift embassage to heaven, only her private bitterness at Angelo is not hollow evasion and cover-up. Both characters speak from fear. He is afraid of death, and she (as she will admit, 73ff.) is afraid that in his desire to live he will not validate the importance to her of her chastity. She generates the suspense about her telling the particulars of the judge's "devilish mercy" so that she can discredit her brother's desiring it in advance. But from the first the emphasis of this persuasion is on this life. The judge's mercy ". . . will free your life, / But fetter you till death" (64–66). He thinks she means life imprisonment, but she explains the justness of his phrase, "perpetual durance," not as we might expect by reference to hell but rather, renewing the scope-restraint opposition, to a restriction of being. Her appeal she makes clear is, as foretold, to his "mind of honour," and when he tautly demands "Let me know the point," she answers from her fear:

> *Isab.*   O, I do fear thee, Claudio, and I quake
> Lest thou a feverous life shouldst entertain,
> And six or seven winters more respect
> Than a perpetual honour.
>
> (73–76)

"Perpetual honour" makes us think of honor before God but only to recognize that the context does not support that emphasis. She provocatively asks "Dar'st thou die?" (76) and would shame him to choose to die by claiming how little death itself, in contrast to apprehension of it, actually hurts. Her lines on the pang of the poor beetle (77–80) are beautiful, though capable of being construed with a force opposite to that which she intends. But all that is very easy for her to say. No one is asking her to die, and for the audience, in position to anticipate, her argument to preserve his honor can hardly be separated from her desire to preserve her own. She succeeds in provoking what sounds like the response she wants.

> *Cla.*   Why give you me this shame?
> Think you I can a resolution fetch
> From flowery tenderness? If I must die,
> I will encounter darkness as a bride
> And hug it in mine arms.
>
> (80–84)

The interest in unconscious verbal self-betrayal in this play is directly proportional to its consideration of "Know thyself," an imperative neither of these characters is fitted to obey. In his situation Claudio could scarcely have chosen deliberately an image that would better expose his resolution as huff-puff. But she is so eagerly gratified to hear in this her father's voice and the nobility she hoped for that she finally confides the perfidy of "this outward-sainted deputy." Yet she does not do so without returning the context to the question of sin and specifying the offense in Claudio inextricably connected to "this rank offence" demanded of her.

> Dost thou think, Claudio,
> If I would yield him my virginity
> Thou mightst be freed?

Cla. O heavens, it cannot be!

Isab. Yes, he would give't thee, from this rank offence,
So to offend him still. This night's the time
That I should do what I abhor to name;
Or else thou diest tomorrow.

Cla. Thou shalt not do't.

(96–102)

The compacted phrase "So to offend him still" has been ill-glossed. It explains the freedom Angelo would give "from this rank offence" as only that for Claudio to continue in the offense for which he has been condemned, for accepting it on such terms would be to turn yet another to fornication. Claudio rejects that like Jehovah on Sinai, and she can hardly not proffer something in return; but it is like a nonswimmer's offer of a check for ten dollars to a drowning man.

Isab. O, were it but my life,
I'd throw it down for your deliverance
As frankly as a pin.

Cla. Thanks, dear Isabel.

Isab. Be ready, Claudio, for your death tomorrow.

Cla. Yes.—Has he affections in him,
That thus can make him bite the law by th'nose
When he would force it?—Sure, it is no sin;
Or of the deadly seven it is the least.

Isab. Which is the least?

Cla. If it were damnable, he being so wise,
Why would he for the momentary trick
Be perdurably fin'd?—O Isabel!

Isab. What says my brother?

Cla. Death is a fearful thing.

Isab. And shamed life a hateful.

Cla. Ay, but to die, and go we know not where; . . .

(103–17)

This fastidious savior would gladly lay down her life for his deliverance, but not her body. His amusing half-abstracted "Thanks" already betrays the wheels turning in his head, for ironically her gratuitous hypothetical offer of selfless sacrifice proves to have prompted him to see the doctrine of deadly sin rather illogically, as it is in earth and not in heaven. That is easily followed by his taking the so-wise Angelo for his exemplar, effectively showing the corrupting consequence of unworthiness in authority. For all the talk of sin, the truth is that neither of them is really thinking of heaven. For her a shamed life is hateful—she is talking of his but she must also be thinking (as we are) of hers. He agrees, but the consideration fades to nothing before what we fear of death.

That speech on death is Claudio's big moment, the answering non-Christian argument, complete with disreputable pagan eschatology,[63] to the Friar's reasoning with life, as well as to his sister's. His passionate utterance brings a rush of descriptive vitality to the poetry with a sweep of ranging imagery that paradoxically liberates the claustrophobic scene, as though the license to name our imagined terrors of the great unknown intensifies the sense of vital human being in the urgent reach of its consciousness, the grandeur and uncertainty of its imaginings.

> To be imprison'd in the viewless winds
> And blown with restless violence round about
> The pendent world:
>
> (123–25)

There is nothing like that elsewhere in the whole play. The speech makes his consequent plea a humiliating comedown, and it quite upstages Isabella until the plea affords her opportunity to set herself up with the force of her own violently rejecting passion and hysterical conceits. The two big speeches climactically express the fears developed from the start of the grouping. Why else enumerate her powers as intercessor, presumed and real, to save by act and word, save to deny them? His terror at the imagined horrors of death evinces her pity, his plea an intense outrage she needs to be overdetermined.

Isab.   Alas, alas!

Cla.   Sweet sister, let me live.
         What sin you do to save a brother's life,

Nature dispenses with the deed so far
That it becomes a virtue.

Isab.   O, you beast!
O faithless coward! O dishonest wretch!
Wilt thou be made a man out of my vice?
Is't not a kind of incest, to take life
From thine own sister's shame? What should I think?
Heaven shield my mother play'd my father fair:
For such a warped slip of wilderness
Ne'er issued from his blood. Take my defiance,
Die, perish! Might but my bending down
Reprieve thee from thy fate, it should proceed.
I'll pray a thousand prayers for thy death:
No word to save thee.

Cla.   Nay hear me, Isabel.

Isab.   O fie, fie, fie!
Thy sin's not accidental, but a trade:
Mercy to thee would prove itself a bawd;
'Tis best that thou diest quickly.   [*Going.*]

Cla.   O hear me, Isabella.

Duke.   [*Advancing.*] Vouchsafe a word, young sister, but
one word.

Isab.   What is your will?

(131–52)

The dispensation of nature that makes sin a virtue of course is
a variation on Angelo's poser about "charity in sin to save this
brother's life." Claudio's appeal, as hers ("What says my
brother?"), is to their natural bond—but also to the corrupt nature
they, and we, share. She sees he wants a travesty of *renovatio*, to
be a man new made out of her vice, that he must be a counterfeit
brother as her name-calling has branded him a counterfeit man.
However hysterical the formulations, there is justice in her insight.
But each has looked for salvation at the hands of the other—and
it is a fleshly salvation both seek, and both are disappointed. In
the weakness in which he has implicated us, he fails to validate
the principle by which she justified her refusal to save him. The
quality of her mercy is that it cannot be strained on a brother's
behalf where her chastity is threatened. There are beams in both
their eyes, but she sees only his. Her denial of the primacy of
charity implicit in her principle is explicitly played out in her merci-

lessly judgmental tirade. The spiritual superiority she aggrandizes makes hers the perfect voice to pronounce the figurative dictum, which here applies literally, that mercy inevitably must prove a bawd to man so corruptly inclined to his own captivity and imprisonment, whose very trade, truly professed, is sin.

Isabella's speech is printed here with what follows to the end of the grouping at the Friar's abrupt reappearance. Most tellingly, it is never quoted that way in criticism of the play, and the Duke's much discussed intervention is considered apart from this context. But here it is, where Claudio at least has not quite finished the scene he and Isabella have played as though alone in the world with their selfhoods and their irreducible problem, and where, significantly, the audience has been awaiting the Duke's reappearance after his overhearing them. The Duke comes forward, with one verse line already modulating into prose, trying to buttonhole the formidable Isabella to listen to one word in parallel with the ignored Claudio's imploring her to hear him. Now, after Isabella's very high dudgeon, that intervention is comic and discharges the crackling tension just after it reaches a *ne plus ultra*. Tillyard amusingly finds in her arrangements to speak with the Duke the "native ferocity" of "the true Isabella" exchanged for the "tones of a well-trained confidential secretary"[64]; but he is yearning for more white-hot poetry from his "independent and inviolate" heroine, not looking to be amused by the Friar's insistent deference and her limited regal complaisance, or the implicit dramatic irony of her "What is your will?" to yet a third male interlocutor. But it is about time the Duke took a responsible hand in the course of events that he, after all, set in motion. He now busily sets to work, dispelling Claudio's fallible hopes and letting him ask his sister's pardon while arranging for the summoned Provost to leave so he may have the stage alone with Isabella. A third function of that short covering speech is accomplished through the attention-getting oddity of its manner.

Cla.   Let me ask my sister pardon; I am so out of love with life that I will sue to be rid of it.

Duke.   Hold you there: farewell.—[*Claudio retires.*] Provost, a word with you.

Prov.   [*advancing*] What's your will, father?

Duke.   That, now you are come, you will be gone. Leave me a while

with the maid; my mind promises with my habit no loss shall
touch her by my company.

Prov.   In good time. *Exit [with Claudio. Isabella comes forward]*.

(170–78)

Commentators are uninterested in this, but the Wife of Bath, two
centuries earlier, would have guffawed at what in the Duke may
pass for dry humor about the lubricity associated with his friar's
habit. The question is why Shakespeare intrudes such a consideration on the attention of his audience. The answer is that it prepares
us to the possibility of viewing the Duke's coming proposition as
the third sexual seduction the chaste heroine undergoes.

He begins of course with flattery that finds grace the soul of her
complexion. But it is flattery that implies at the same time a critique of her rigid stance, for with that grace from a God who regards our hearts, her essential chastity in yielding to Angelo to
save her brother might remain untouched. To hear her "goodness"
extolled so soon after her furious firing for effect on her much
barraged brother assures that we do not miss that it is flattery.
Which means he wants her to do something. Having evinced from
her how she plans to conclude the action, which as drama would
be (as theater-man Shakespeare might say) mere nothing, he begins
to unfold the elements of a desired comic conclusion she could
bring about. He sees a remedy—what everyone has been talking
about but not been able to come by, and it will "redeem" her
brother from the angry law and "do no stain to your own gracious
person": "to the love I have in doing good, a remedy presents
itself" (197ff.).[65] That is the way it usually is quoted. But what
immediately follows deliberately sticks a fly in the ointment: "I do
make myself believe that you may most uprighteously do. . . ."
Why alert us this way if, as numerous writers would have us believe, his plan is to be viewed as entirely kosher? Another opinion
widely held (by very different critics) is that Shakespeare has suddenly abandoned here the Isabella he created. But the Isabella who
responds to the Duke's come-on is very Isabella indeed in her
courage and self-consciously high-principled reserve.

Isab.   Let me hear you speak farther. I have spirit to do anything
that appears not foul in the truth of my spirit.

(205–7)

That will make her contentment with the remedy (260–61) the more interesting if it prove in its well-intended end as well as means not quite 100 percent kosher (which of course is not kosher at all).

He softens her response with the sweet and sour story of another maiden unjustly treated by "this well-seeming Angelo" (223), meanwhile arresting us with the disclosure of the depth in time of his own dark purpose in the action. The sentimental tableau in rhythmic prose concluding his tale disarms her to an amusing and charming disclosure of herself.

> *Isab.* Can this be so? Did Angelo so leave her?
>
> *Duke.* Left her in her tears, and dried not one of them with his comfort: swallowed his vows whole, pretending in her discoveries of dishonour: in few, bestowed her on her own lamentation, which she yet wears for his sake; and he, a marble to her tears, is washed with them, but relents not.
>
> *Isab.* What a merit were it in death to take this poor maid from the world! What corruption in this life, that it will let this man live!
>
> (224–33)

She is, under all that armor, intelligence, and theory, a naïf—and a romantic to boot, with a solution for all problems that would indeed end them, but not as comedy would hope or the Duke's remedy propose. Where she sees two deaths, the remedymaker shows her "a rupture that you may easily heal: and the cure of it not only saves your brother, but keeps you from dishonour in doing it" (235–37). This latter assurance, iterated several times in the course of their dialogue by this benevolent father figure, steadies her to ask and be told the how of it. This is the tricky part and his procedure is fascination. First he tells of the jilted maid's continuing, and now yet more violent and unruly love, then abruptly shifts to the present directives for Isabella's pretended yielding to Angelo, holding in suspense how her agreement with his demands is to be fulfilled: "and now follows all." He switches to the absolute future to say how only then she and he together "shall advise this wronged maid to stead up your appointment, go in your place" (250–51). Summarizing the desirable consequences to follow from that encounter, which now include "the corrupt deputy scaled" (255–56)—weighed in the balance to be found wanting—the dis-

guised deputy concludes by authoritatively encouraging her participating concurrence in the justification for it he proffers.

> If you think well to carry this as you may, the
> doubleness of the benefit defends the deceit from reproof.
> What think you of it?

Isab. The image of it gives me content already, and I trust it will
grow to a most prosperous perfection.

(257–61)

He further challenges her enthusiasm for its "prosperous perfection" by emphasizing how much that depends on her: "It lies much
in your holding up [O irresistible puns!] . . . if for this night he
entreat you to his bed, give him promise of satisfaction" (261–64).
She ends with what surely is an invitation to us to savor an irony
by thanking the "good father" from whom spiritual comfort might
be hoped "for this comfort" (269–70).

"What think you of it?" as it is a question also put before the
audience, shows that those who would sterilize this bed-trick by
referring us to the opaque neutrality of the conventional motif in
story are hiding their heads in the sand.[66] Those offended by Isabella's contentment with the plan, who would charge Shakespeare
with abandoning the dramatic character earlier represented, betray
an interest in preserving their heroine intact from the revelation
of his character's complex inconsistency ongoing from her first
word in his play. On the other hand, those pleased to condemn her
for assisting another to do what she abhorred to do herself may
be charged with imprecision, for Mariana's proposed intercourse
with Angelo is not the same thing. Mariana has claim on Angelo
and by bedding him can claim title to him. What Isabella may be
charged with is the unconscious hypocrisy of preserving her honor
untainted by being accessory to what was sin in Juliet and Claudio.
Our queasiness about the Friar's remedy is warranted because he
is not fully candid about the means that the beneficial ends justify,
or indeed about the ends. He is made to cite "the doubleness of
the benefit" (when by his own account it is quadruple) because
there is deceit in it. But the problem is located here only by the
irony that is emphasized by their costumes. Shakespeare post-
pones until the moated grange scene the direct confrontation of it.
What he does not postpone is consideration of the other point

Isabel is unconscious of, in this matter of getting a woman to go to bed as another with a man to whom she is not quite married. By redeeming her brother with this remedy, she is showing indeed that mercy to him would prove itself a bawd. Since the Duke-Friar concocted the remedy, it is only fair that, as Isabella goes off to her meeting with Angelo, he be left to take the heat as this point is announced through dramatic action by Elbow's entrance with the arrested Pompey the bawd in tow.

> *Elbow.* Nay, if there be no remedy for it, but that you will needs buy and sell men and women like beasts, we shall have all the world drink brown and white bastard.
>
> (III.ii.1–4)

Much virtue in Elbow, the arresting officer, much virtue in "it." As the Friar with unconscious propriety says, at last, "O heavens, what stuff is here?"

* * *

This scene is but half over at Isabella's exit, half its voices yet to be heard, and these are to liberate the scene for broader comic perspective, largely at the expense of authority as in II.i; and also to widen its reference, as in Pompey's complaint that the greater usury is allowed by order of law or in the Friar's incisive news of the world that is every day's news (6–10; 215–24). The seven groupings comprising this half of the scene are quite unrequired by the main plot, one version of whose essence the Duke neatly distills: "There is so great a fever on goodness that the dissolution of it must cure it" (216–17). But we do get late exposition about Lucio crucial to his appearance as the one character associated with the lowlifes to be included in the finale. However, what these groupings concentrate on that is quite essential is clarification of the Duke. Shakespeare exposes him to a series of imagings of himself—differently distortive, and hilarity- and thought-provoking as the images of a self in a sequence of funhouse mirrors—in order to arrive finally at a more balanced, if still removed, view of him in his concluding soliloquy.

First there is the old trick of having him joke at the level of Elbow's greeting.

Elbow. Come your way, sir.—Bless you, good father friar.

Duke. And you, good brother father. What offence hath this man
   made you, sir?

                                                    (11–13)

He is then further analogized by the arrested Pompey, on whom
the officers have found "a strange picklock" (16)—an identifying
instrument doubtless for opening chastity belts (actual or figurative). The Friar with some heat and revulsion castigates the bawd,
laying bare what it literally is to take one's living from the sexual
sins of others. But the moral superiority to the bawd is eroded as
soon as Pompey tries to justify his living despite its stink, in prose
set against the Friar's verse.

Duke. Fie, sirrah, a bawd, a wicked bawd;
   The evil that thou causest to be done,
   That is thy means to live. Do thou but think
   What 'tis to cram a maw or clothe a back
   From such a filthy vice. Say to thyself,
   From their abominable and beastly touches
   I drink, I eat, array myself, and live.
   Canst thou believe thy living is a life,
   So stinkingly depending? Go mend, go mend.

Pom. Indeed it does stink in some sort, sir. But yet, sir, I would
   prove—

Duke. Nay, if the devil have given thee proofs for sin,
   Thou wilt prove his. Take him to prison, officer:
   Correction and instruction must both work
   Ere this rude beast will profit.

                                                    (18–32)

"Proofs for sin" are devilish mimicry of "proofs" from Holy Writ
in support of theological propositions. Elbow assures the Friar that
the bawd won't get away with it this time. He must appear before
"the deputy" who "cannot abide a whoremaster" (33–34). The
Duke's general comment, thinking of Angelo, is so made as to
reflect on himself.

Duke. That we were all, as some would seem to be,
   From our faults, as faults from seeming, free!

                                                    (37–38)

That there is in the bawd a tie-in with the Friar, Elbow makes clear in his comment on Pompey closing the grouping: "His neck will come to your waist—a cord, sir" (39). That is, he will have a cord around his neck as you, Friar, have one around your waist. To spell that out, with the Friar's expostulations fresh in mind, we are shifted to a different analogue and have the bawd put down and spelled out by the very spokesman for and practitioner of sexual license. Lucio in full flow mocks his captive old acquaintance, refuses to bail him, familiarly rehearsing the perennial inevitabilities of the brothel world, and creating it with his language. Here is the knowing accuser, gustily enjoying the plight he has helped to promote—a "Lucio" in short living up to the diabolic side of his import; for accuser, and slanderer, are the meanings of the devil's name, as the Elizabethans never tire of explaining. Lucio pretends not to know what this familiar prisoner is in for, and evinces from the poor fellow who would live the memorably disconsolate admission, "For being a bawd, for being a bawd" (63). For thirty-five lines the Friar, with but one line ("Still thus, and thus: still worse!" [51]), stands shaking his head at "the trick of it" (50)—the way of the world. But as Pompey is taken off, turning, still hoping Lucio will be his bail, Lucio continues casting cracks at him after already initiating converse with the Friar—so the Duke is neatly caught unhappily wedged between them.

The compulsively loose-tongued Lucio is the most amusingly forgivable Blatant Beast in Elizabethan literature, though Shakespeare is at pains to limn him more darkly with Mrs. Overdone's accusation that he has vengefully informed on her after she was caring for the child he had by Mistress Kate Keepdown (192–97). Only Shakespeare could so deftly at once unexpectedly humanize the bawd and sharply illuminate Lucio. Lucio's dialogue with the Duke, which makes as surefire a comic scene as Kinesias and Myrrhine's, takes off from that familiar excruciation of social existence, the endured unwanted conversation. The very assumption of the propriety of their association and converse, which Lucio so thoroughly enjoys as he seeks to impress and if possible to scandalize the Friar about the Duke, itself hilariously carries the point— and it still does even though we do not bring to it the Elizabethans' sense of degree. Lucio cannot help trying to top himself, banking ever higher the fire to burn him later; meanwhile, the Duke as Friar is for now as defenseless as Lucio is ignorant of his identity.

Eventually indeed he threatens telling on Lucio when the Duke returns but, preserving his disguise, backs off with a taunt ("You'll forswear this again" [161]) that only invites yet bolder calumny from the irrepressible debunker of his Grace.

The Duke can protest, but in his disguise—which we are therefore potently aware of as a disguise—he is powerless to gainsay either Lucio's denigration, or what is harder to take, his approbation, or what is most interesting to ponder, their connection. Lucio resentfully objects, "It was a mad, fantastical trick of him to steal from the state and usurp the beggary he was never born to"— and to leave Lord Angelo to "put transgression to't," particularly lechery (89–95). The Friar repeats the Duke on the "most biting laws": "It is too general a vice, and severity must cure it" (96). But Lucio's sarcasm, whose point we are bound to acknowledge, affords authority no hiding place there.

> *Lucio.* Yes, in good sooth, the vice is of a great kindred; it is well
> allied; but it is impossible to extirp it quite, friar, till eating
> and drinking be put down.
>
> (97–99)

Lucio's playful fantasies about the making of that frigid "motion ungenerative" Angelo (99–108), developed next with the Duke-Friar comically serving as Lucio's "feed," are all the funnier for Lucio's ignorance of the deputy's ungoverned lust that ironically proves his point. *Their* point is actually to set up the contrast with the absent merciful Duke. There is the crux of the matter, and Shakespeare will have Lucio repeat it before his exit (170ff.).

> *Lucio.* Why, what a ruthless thing is this in him, for the rebellion of
> a codpiece to take away the life of a man! Would the Duke
> that is absent have done this? Ere he would have hanged a
> man for the getting a hundred bastards, he would have paid
> for the nursing a thousand. He had some feeling of the sport;
> he knew the service; and that instructed him to mercy.
>
> (110–17)

That is the argument familiar from the Isabella-Angelo scenes: we can be instructed to mercy only through acknowledgement of our own frailty. Lucio simply flies freely on the assumption that we come by such acknowledgement by experience. The Duke was lenient; he must therefore know "the service." The Friar briefly challenges with cool equanimity the slanders of the Duke as a lecher and drunk, but when this self-proclaimed "inward" of his sets up for deflation the opinion of "the greater file of the subject" that the Duke was wise—

> *Duke.* Wise? Why, no question but he was.
>
> *Lucio.* A very superficial, ignorant, unweighing fellow—
>
> *Duke.* Either this is envy in you, folly, or mistaking. The very stream of his life, and the business he hath helmed, must upon a warranted need give him a better proclamation. Let him be but testimonied in his own bringings-forth, and he shall appear to the envious a scholar, a statesman, and a soldier. Therefore you speak unskillfully: or, if your knowledge be more, it is much darkened in your malice.
>
> (132–44)

However just his claims, the Duke can only seem less and less faintly ridiculous the longer he eulogizes himself. The ideal of the Prince he would claim that the Duke embodies seems slightly old-fashioned and vaguely irrelevant to the world in which the Friar defends him. But the big point here surely is the fact that the Duke has been touched in his *amour propre*. Figures of the Deity, including supposed literary incarnations of Divine Providence, do not have an *amour propre* to be wounded. It often has been objected of the reclusive "Duke of dark corners" that for so central a character he remains strangely unparticularized, though indications are plentiful that to create just such a character was the challenge deliberately taken up by the dramatist. Here Shakespeare has succeeded in humanizing the Duke without particularizing him. Moreover, if he is vulnerable he is also, though hardly as this self-discrediting scandal-monger would caricature him in clay, humanly imperfect, subject to blame, and even as here incompletely in control. The comic powerlessness of the Duke as Friar in his dialogue with Lucio leads to his recognition in brief soliloquy that "No might nor greatness in mortality / Can censure 'scape" as well as that the whitest virtue would not protect it from calumny: "What king so strong / Can tie the gall up in the slanderous tongue?" (179–82) Those limitations of his potency cannot be shrugged off as he ignores Lucio's imputation that the lecherous

Duke is "now past it" (176). The entrance now of the arrested Overdone and the exasperated Escalus, reminding us of the Duke's former leniency, emphasizes that in coping with his intractable "subject" the deputy of the Lord is left to strive humanly with the equally intractable problem of weighing severity and leniency, justice and mercy, of finding a measure for measure.[67]

The entrance of Escalus allows the Friar to be reintroduced in verse as "a brother / Of gracious order, late come from the See / In special business from his Holiness" (212–14)—a most ambiguously oblique glance at "knewe ye not that I must go about my fathers business?" (Luke 2:49).[68] This wry onlooker's telling of the "news abroad i' th' world" that certainly could be Jacobean—and, in its comments on venture capitalism substituted for true fellowship in societies, could be ours (220–24)—serves to rehabilitate the Friar as Escalus serves to rehabilitate the Duke. He is now reported "a gentleman of all temperance" and "One that above all other strifes, contended especially to know himself" (226–31). The results of that strife are very much in evidence in the Duke-Friar's choral soliloquy in rhyming verse that gives a point of ordered formality to conclude this dramatic movement. The speech used to be much deplored, even supposed non-Shakespearean, but its rhyming short lines and terse sententious observation make an arresting change of pace and have an authoritative intensity that does come from the Duke and the context.[69] The speech is in four equal parts by subject, the third obscure with an obvious two-line hiatus; but the first offers a basis in principle for both the indignation at Angelo's misrule and the concluding return to the bed-trick, that considers his plan to counter Angelo's vice.

> He who the sword of heaven will bear
> Should be as holy as severe:
> Pattern in himself to know,
> Grace to stand, and virtue, go:
> More nor less to others paying
> Than by self-offences weighing.
>
> (254–59)

"Pattern," significantly, here means precedent, not a model for imitation, as Lever has well glossed: "To know that the precedent for his judgement lies in his own conduct." The Duke, who knows that one must stand before he can walk and that the ruler needs grace to stand and virtue to go, again acknowledges "my vice," owning that which he had allowed to flourish; but he does so hotly to invoke "Twice treble shame on Angelo, / To weed my vice, and let his grow!" (262–63) Against his deputy's disguise and "practice" the bearer of the sword of heaven flatly says he "must apply" craft (270), and then folds the bed-trick substitution into rhyming lines that pose measure against measure, disguise against disguise, falsehood against the "false exacting" of Angelo's extortion, to end with the fulfillment of "an old contracting" of marriage already vowed (271–75). His reference to the legalities of *sponsalia de futuro* shows that he speaks of the matter as secular ruler. That is carefully distinguished by contrast with his costume here, and with what he will say of it as Friar at the close of the next scene.

The verse form that startles us in this speech is of course most often used for prologues and epilogues, and the big crosscut now to the song of the moated grange scene makes this soliloquy seem to have been prologous. And indeed the part of the action embarked upon concerns the crucial substitutions, hoped for and unexpected, needed for the Duke's rescue of the situation. The shift of locale from the prison is a relief, though it is short lived, and in fact Mariana in the moated grange, arrested in her woeful forsaken love ("I have sat here all day" [IV.i.19–20]), is a kind of prisoner awaiting enfranchisement too. Even the exquisite song she explains thus: "it . . . pleas'd my woe" (13). The air of romance breathed into the play is already transpiring into something else with the Friar's comment on music in reply.

> *Duke.*   'Tis good; though music oft hath such a charm
> To make bad good, and good provoke to harm.
>
>   (14–15)

That comment—on the seductive power to make bad seem good and so endanger virtue—for us cannot but relate to the business of the scene: the enlisting of Mariana as Isabella's substitute at the assignation the Duke has prompted and Isabella has arranged.[70] The to and fro-ing of the scene assures that its focus is not on Mariana (who, it will shortly be stressed, knows not "a word of this" [50]), but more interestingly, and safely, and to different ends, first on Isabella and then on the Duke. Isabella's recital of her arrangement with Angelo—a scene wonderful to have played if the play were hers—vividly implicates her in the rendezvous. After the Friar prepares Mariana to listen to her story ("Do you persuade yourself that I respect you?" [53]), she is the one who informs Mariana and speaks for her her response to the proposition when they reenter. The Duke's answer is the climax and conclusion of the scene. It concerns his implication in the substitution and it is prepared for by the focus on him in his brief soliloquy that serves as covering speech while the women, who have "walk[ed] aside," entertain the proposal.

> [Mariana *and* Isabella *withdraw.*]
>
> *Duke.* O place and greatness! Millions of false eyes
> Are stuck upon thee: volumes of report
> Run with these false, and most contrarious quest
> Upon thy doings: thousand escapes of wit
> Make thee the father of their idle dream
> And rack thee in their fancies.
>
> (59–65)

Since Warburton, the notion has recurred that these lines "are absolutely foreign to the subject of the scene" and properly belong, as Mary Lascelles reconstructs the text, at the start of the observations on calumny occasioned by Lucio in the previous scene. Though he does not emend and admits a monologue is needed, Lever concurs. His idea, like Dover Wilson's, that these lines are "insufficient to provide for the interval" required, betrays an inappropriately literal expectation of Shakespearean verisimilitude. The assertions that "the lines . . . have been transferred from the Duke's earlier soliloquy" and that they "are irrelevant in their context" are quite erroneous.[71] Of course the lines connect with the Lucio business in the previous scene. The dramatic point of the earlier provocation to reflect on calumny is to be more tightly considered here. There the audience had the substitution in prospect; here it is crucially amaking, and it is entirely appropriate for the Duke to speak as the Duke with a new emphasis on eagerly hostile misinterpretations of his doings. Greatness, with so many falsely seeing eyes fixed on it, is dogged by accordant misrepresenting reports of its doings, and its identity fancifully tortured out of shape for sallies of wit that falsely claim its paternity for their most unlike "idle dream." "Father" (64) is a neat trick, as the Duke is operative in these doings in his Friar's disguise, and "father" is what he will next be called (66). The audience is fairly admonished not to "contrarious quest" upon the Duke's doings. And then what does he do when Isabella and an agreeable Mariana have been greeted by his advice and entreaty to "take the enterprise upon her" (66–68)?

> *Isab.*   Little have you to say
> When you depart from him, but, soft and low,
> 'Remember now my brother'.
>
> *Mariana.*   Fear me not.
>
> *Duke.* Nor, gentle daughter, fear you not at all.
> He is your husband on a pre-contract:
> To bring you thus together 'tis no sin,
> Sith that the justice of your title to him
> Doth flourish the deceit.—Come, let us go;
> Our corn's to reap, for yet our tithe's to sow.
>
> (68–76)

Now that is a big stretcher. And how convenient, as well as emphatic and effective, to conclude with it, finessing any chance of Isabella's crying "Hold!" as well she might, for she should know better. It is a fair treat to watch Christian interpreters trying to evade or argue away this speech. But the deceit the speech flourishes trumpetlike is in its logic. The justice of Mariana's title to Angelo may embellish or grace the deceit of her coming to him as Isabella, but it scarcely follows that because of *that* "to bring you thus together is no sin." Of course this intercourse, lacking the blessing of ceremonious marriage, is as much a sin as Claudio and Juliet's, as well as reasonable cause for defamation of her character. Why else publicly have them sent off to be married by real Friar Peter before the Duke condemns Angelo? But there is a good deal more to the problematic here than that.

Marriage contracted *de futuro,* such as was Angelo and Mariana's, was a matter of common law. It could be and often was encumbered with conditions. The Duke's account to Isabella of Angelo's denying his contracted bride of course is romantic and sentimental. Though homilists inveighed against marriage for financial or economic gain, sensible Elizabethans were minded otherwise. If, as often was the case, a specified dowry was a condition of the promise to wed, then the loss of Mariana's dowry gave Angelo clear legal right to consider his obligation under the contract null. There was an exception that in common law removed any such condition, namely, consummation of the marriage. But the reasoning here is crucial: "'For . . . it is always presupposed, that a mutuall consent, as touching Marriage, hath gone before.'"[72] That is not the case here; indeed, Schanzer points out that Angelo could under English common law challenge the contract because of the substitution of the partners.[73] But the issue in the play is more searching. Mariana is consummating her marriage in having intercourse with Angelo. In having sex with her, Angelo is doing nothing of the sort. He supposes he is having intercourse with Isabella, and of course that is a sin. The Duke in soliloquy later, when the messenger arrives bearing what he supposes must be Claudio's pardon, is quite specific on that point: "This is his pardon, purchas'd by such sin / For which the pardoner himself is in" (IV.ii.106–7). When the Friar says here, "To bring you thus together is no sin,"—and "you" is surely plural—we hear the Duke who admitted he must use "Craft against vice" (III.ii.270). To take a device of story and put it through such scrutiny is most typical of this play. God, we are told over and over by Elizabethan religious writers, "examineth the heart and the reins." For the Duke to assure Mariana that there is no sin in bringing them together "thus"—by a deceit pretending that a man committing a mortal sin in the act is fulfilling a contract through consummation requiring mutual consent—is a whopper. Not to see that is to be ill-prepared for the delightful logic in the Duke's condemning Angelo to death in part for violation of sacred chastity when he reenters after being ordered to be married instantly to Mariana because he was contracted to her!

So much, then, for romance. Indeed, we are immediately returned to the prison, and it is surely by no accident, but rather by way of analogical preparation for the Duke's next doings, that we have the "notorious bawd" Pompey turned into the executioner's assistant. Abhorson the executioner, comically concerned for the credit of "our mystery" (26–27), is affronted by this association. But the Provost, who calls both "sirrah," dismissively tells him, "You weigh equally: a feather will turn the scale"; and their comically coming to agreement in equivalent claims for their professions as "mysteries" bears him out: one sells falsehood, the other is a thief (28–45). Indeed, they are so much "agreed,"[74] it is equivocal whether in offering Abhorson "a good turn" if he has occasion to use him for a good turn (54–57), Pompey is speaking of sex or hanging. All this is also preparation for the Provost's calling hither another pair, another sexual offender (and "bawd") and another sort of taker of men's lives—Claudio and Barnardine. Under the absoluteness of the law, both are to be executed, but they are differentiated, first in the manner important from the play's second scene (129) by the Provost in soliloquy—"Th'one has my pity; not a jot the other, / Being a murderer, though he were my brother" (59–60)—and next in their response to the summons to be shown the warrants for their deaths. Claudio appears so he may be told "prepare yourself" (67); Barnardine does not: "He will not wake" (66). Ironically, Claudio describes him (64–65) as in the sleep of the innocent worker (Eccles. 5:12). Barnardine is dropped from our attention until later with the start of the routine of knocking within combined with onstage hope of the arrival of "some pardon or reprieve / For the most gentle Claudio" (69–70). But this context alone, certainly for the original audience, makes a spiritual contrast. The Christian is enjoined spiritually not to sleep; for one cannot be prepared to live or die unless he be spiritually awake.[75]

The suspense so carefully built about the arrival of Claudio's pardon seems, because of the expectation shared by the audience with the Duke, of the easy sort that gratifies those in the know with superiority to those who expectantly wait the same outcome—but are, as the Provost is, on tenterhooks losing hope. When the surprise comes finally with the reading of Angelo's missive mocking expectation, the Duke, who has just confidently moralized on the pardon in a six-line soliloquy (106–11), is abandoned by us to suffer the entire deflation because the know-it-all misled us. What moderates the effect of this exposure of his lack of omniscience is, first, the very fact that his worldliness was not so cynical as to imagine that Angelo's depravity would reach to such treachery, and second, his turning from the disappointment with unruffled aplomb to inquire about this Barnardine, now carefully delineated in advance of his appearance in the next scene. Barnardine is a character essential to the play as a limiting case, to put all others in perspective. His liberty is that of the prison, granted because he would not escape even given leave to do so. Insentience of his own humanity is the hallmark of this ultimate prisoner condemned to death. His confirmed taking of a human life depicts his drunken existence, in which he has as little apprehension of death as care of what is past, present, or to come. In the Provost's summation: "insensible of mortality, and desperately mortal" (142–43)—that is, without hope of being anything but mortal. After that accolade, the Friar's "He needs advice" gets a brief laugh because it sounds like a Band–Aid: the point is that Barnardine "will hear none" (144–45).

"But more of him anon" as the Duke says, going to work manipulating to his will the Provost, whom he flatters for having "honesty and constancy" written in his brow. Ironically, the assessment proves correct. The Friar finds that "neither my coat, integrity, nor persuasion can with ease attempt" (188–89) the Provost from his sworn duty; he is a foil for his vow- and promise-breaking superior, the deputy. So the Duke must go further than he meant to (189–90) and finally tip his hand. Against Angelo's note, to guarantee the Duke will acknowledge the justice of the Provost's dealing, he sets the hand and seal of the Duke on the letter whose "contents . . . is the return of the Duke" (195). The phrase "with ease" refers to the fact that the Duke's improvising has been played out, with many time references, against a fast clock. At line 62 it is midnight; at the very end "it is almost clear dawn" (209). Just before that, the Duke-Friar injects a pastoral note in stirring the amazed Provost to call his executioner and off with Barnardine's required head: "Look, th'unfolding star calls up the shepherd" (202–3). Amidst these contrary tones, this shepherd goes off to give Barnardine a short and "present shrift." The close would seem to mark an emergence into daylight (like Don Pedro's ending of the Monument Scene in *Much Ado*). But by this point we are wise to this play and expect to be gratified by no such thing. We are not disappointed.

The crosscut returns us to Pompey, who has discovered that he is as well acquainted in prison as he was "in our house of profession"; most of his customers are here, as he illustrates with a colorful sampling, with type-names, of the roisterers, men about town pretenders, bankrupts, gamblers, phony blusterers of honor, sports, and bawd-gallants—all cheaters or cheated, all, as Pompey says, "great doers [that is, copulators] in our trade" (IV.iii.1–20). It is as though the crackdown under Vienna's laws (evocative of some recent English edicts) had swept up Jacobean London's riffraff, though the idea that the devisers of the Statute of Stabbing (1604) had in mind the remanding of "wild Half-can that stabbed pots" presumably to serve mismarked measures of ale mocks the pretension of such governmental measures. *Wild Half-can* most likely alludes to James's proclamation "for the reformation of great abuses in Measures" (1 June 1603), which ordered the standards of measurement varying throughout the kingdom brought in line with the authoritative set in London. Paul Hammond, without reference to this passage, has insightfully suggested that "If Shakespeare was a thoughtful observer of these royal attempts to enforce new standards, then he may have reflected on the metaphorical overtones of James's Proclamation" insisting on an authoritative measure of measures.[76]

Through Pompey, the bawdy house—as the convent more delicately earlier and more indelicately here (another "house of profession")—is seen in the same frame with the prison. Of course it is ironic at Angelo's expense, and that of Justice, that the bawd should now be an executioner. But the irony is trained round to bear on the Duke-Friar in Pompey's first assignment, on which Shakespeare expends an entire grouping to build up Barnardine's entrance. The whole routine of his "friends, the executioner" to get the sleeping Barnardine "to rise up and be put to death," funny in itself, is much more pointedly comic for an audience with spiritual sleep and waking in mind; and of course we should have it in mind because the Friar is on his way and the whole next grouping employs the three characters in ensemble to roll out a carpet for his entrance.

Pom.	Pray, Master Barnadine, awake till you are executed, and sleep afterwards.
Abhor.	Go in to him and fetch him out.
Pom.	He is coming, sir, he is coming. I hear his straw rustle.

Enter Barnardine.

Abhor.	Is the axe upon the block, sirrah?
Pom.	Very ready, sir.
Barnardine.	How now, Abhorson? What's the news with you?

Abhor.   Truly, sir, I would desire you to clap into your prayers;
               for look you, the warrant's come.

Barnardine. You rogue, I have been drinking all night; I am not
               fitted for't.

Pom.   O, the better, sir; for he that drinks all night, and is
               hanged betimes in the morning, may sleep the sounder
               all the next day.

               Enter Duke [*disguised*].

Abhor.   Look you, sir, here comes your ghostly father. Do we
               jest now, think you?

Duke.   Sir, induced by my charity, I am come to advise you,
               comfort you, and pray with you.

                                                        (31–51)

An acquaintance of the writer's who once played Barnardine
used to drink a warm bottle of Pepsi-Cola before each performance
so he could produce a resounding eructation before his entrance.
For Shakespeare, Pompey's vivid reference to the straw rustling
suffices to introduce the incarnation of the beast-man so talked of
in the play. Audiences eat him up, and since it actually has been
doubted "whether the qualities that have made him deathless in
the imagination [of many readers] were part of Shakespeare's design," even supposed that he is spared because he so endeared
himself to his maker that he had not the heart to use him for the
substitution for which he had created him,[77] the why and wherefore
of the delight in Barnardine deserve consideration. The Provost
has spared us any temptation to pity the murderer; he never would
be missed, so we can start as indifferent to his death as he is and
enjoy him. Our laughter at his protest that he is on his own terms
"not fitted" for his death (though Pompey shows he paradoxically
is) is cathartic because he reflects us. His flat statement in a moment to the Friar, "I will have more time to prepare me" (53) is
what Everyman wants, asserted as a right, quite without the fear
that makes worldling Everyman at his summoning try to wheedle.
Barnardine makes death a matter of consent (55), and we love him
for it. To this figure enter the phony Friar with his brisk holy
purpose—not to prepare for death a man he intends to save but
one who not only is really about to die but whose death the "Friar"

urgently requires. The Duke can be no more disinterested in fitting this fellow man's mind to death than Isabel was with her brother. This action is pendent to that one and farcically so because the Duke wants Barnardine executed so he can have his head. (The head-maidenhead connection of I.ii Pompey has refreshed when first approached about being an executioner [IV.ii.3–4].) Of course we are with Barnardine when, by frustrating the Duke's purpose, he causes him literally to expose himself to the laughter of comedy, and to the recognition of the limits of his power.

Barnardine. I swear I will not die today for any man's persuasion.

Duke. But hear you—

Barnardine. Not a word. If you have anything to say to me, come to my ward: for thence will not I today.

Exit.

Enter Provost.

Duke. Unfit to live or die! O gravel heart.
After him, fellows, bring him to the block!
[*Exeunt* Abhorson *and* Pompey.]

Prov. Now sir, how do you find the prisoner?

Duke. A creature unprepar'd, unmeet for death;
And to transport him in the mind he is
Were damnable.

(58–68)

In the new Arden, following Dr. Johnson's conjecture and privately persuaded by Nevill Coghill (whose view of the Duke could not accommodate what is going on here), Lever reassigned line 64, the shout to the fellows, to the Provost.[78] To be sure, "it is incongruous for the Duke as Friar to shout orders to the executioners"; that it is the Duke in the disguise who is shouting at them is what makes the comic climax; and that is intellectual farce. To suppose their drift "absurdly contradicts his comment in 63 and his opinion in 66–8" is to read backwards on behalf of a consistency critically imposed. Their drift absurdly contradicts his comment in 63 only as seen in the light of the realization in 66–68. Again, Lever sees that 65, the Provost's line in the Folio, is an ironic "I told you so" but does not see that throwing in 64 contradicts that. The Provost has no urgency to say that line. He has come to tell of Ragozine's death; he has a head like Claudio's to hand, and he is about to propose that they "omit / This reprobate"—scheduled to die this afternoon—"until he were well inclin'd" (72–73). The Duke, and we, discover that human authority has very real limits, particularly in regard to the individual's right to live (as Lever appreciates). The Duke is no more God-like in potency than he was God-like in omniscience, and this play emphatically makes that quite as important a discovery as that complementary one announced in the Duke's relieved exclamation on hearing of the availability of this Claudio-like head: "O, 'tis an accident that heaven provides" (76).

Things promise to move more swiftly now in a pattern of ducal orders—soliloquy—order—soliloquy, with the Provost obediently going off, on, and off again as told. But we are not yet off the roller coaster. Having got the Provost off for the head to be sent to Angelo, the Duke in soliloquy becomes increasingly decisive in his envisioned control of events to come as he plans his public return from a point outside the city. "And from thence" he promises, switching to the royal pronoun, "By cold gradation and well-balanc'd form, / We shall proceed with Angelo" (98–100). In this we are altogether with the Duke. But after the Provost reappears and leaves with the head, Isabella's call within, announcing her arrival in expectation of news of Claudio's pardon, provokes another soliloquy, sharing his plans for her, and that surprises us into distance from him. Here is the one place in the play where the Duke expressly conceives of himself as playing at God, and after what has gone before in this scene and the last, that has to be flabbergasting.

Enter Provost.

Prov. Here is the head; I'll carry it myself.

Duke. Convenient is it. Make a swift return;
For I would commune with you of such things
That want no ear but yours.

Prov.   I'll make all speed. *Exit.*

Isab. [*within.*] Peace, hoa, be here!

Duke. The tongue of Isabel. She's come to know

If yet her brother's pardon be come hither;
But I will keep her ignorant of her good,
To make her heavenly comforts of despair
When it is least expected.

> *Enter* Isabella.

Isab.   Hoa, by your leave!

Duke.   Good morning to you, fair and gracious daughter.

Isab.   The better, given me by so holy a man.

                                                    (101–12)

The Duke has been laboring to get credible means to make Angelo believe his perfidious order has been obeyed and Claudio is dead. The Provost's entry with the property head—which (I think) should look indeed like Claudio's—momentarily gives that apparent truth a shocking factuality. Given the momentum of the Duke's thought of that anticipated proceeding with Angelo, we may (if we are quick) realize it would be most convenient for Isabella to be as disappointed about the pardon as the Duke was, so that the accuser will bring the same conviction of Claudio's death to the proceeding as the accused. And this idea indeed is picked up later when the Friar advises her "to the head of Angelo / Accuse him home and home" (142–43). But the Duke does not talk of that here, but rather of Isabella's "heavenly comforts" from his untruth to her that withholds "her good." The signals in his speech appear contradictory. "The tongue of Isabel" sounds curiously closely engaged: he has never called her that. But the hybristic-sounding plan seems insensitively manipulative. The despair and comforts clearly have to do with more than the fact of which he plans to keep her in ignorance; but we do not know what they are to justify the trial of his pain-inflicting lie. If he is going to turn her into some sort of Griselda or correct her through adversity like God, he ought to have the powers truly to warrant the apparent cruelty of imposing actual suffering, for the claim is that his earthly manipulation will produce genuinely "heavenly comforts." But he has been shown by the preceding action to lack the divine attributes to warrant such a claim. The pattern of the action would seem to invite us, rather, to expect his exposure as unequal to such a role. Her greeting of the Friar boldly confirms that expectation; but his greeting of her could propose an exposure of her too. Shakespeare has framed things so that an audience will be fiercely attentive to her response to that lie, and watchful for what the Duke has in mind to alter in her to see why the lie conceivably might be for her good. The surprise here depends on the fact that the Duke in his Friar's costume knows he is in disguise. The sister in her garb does not yet have a glimmer that she might be in disguise. That part of the parallelism in action with the self-ignorant Angelo has not yet been brought home to her. Ironically, the beginning of that process is abetted at the expense of that "so holy a man," the Friar. The brilliance of this grouping in the scene depends on its relation to the climax preceding. There the figure comically exposed was not the Friar, but the Duke. Here the figure exposed clearly is the Friar, not the Duke. The Duke may mean "heavenly comforts" still.

His intentions are partly defined by turning the Friar's upside-down proposals to her right side up. The Friar begins holily enough.

> Hath yet the deputy sent my brother's pardon?
>
> *Duke.* He hath releas'd him, Isabel,—from the world.
> His head is off, and sent to Angelo.
>
> *Isab.* Nay, but it is not so!
>
> *Duke.* It is no other. Show your wisdom, daughter,
> In your close patience.
>
> *Isab.* O, I will to him and pluck out his eyes!
>
> *Duke.* You shall not be admitted to his sight.
>
> *Isab.* Unhappy Claudio! wretched Isabel!
> Injurious world! most damned Angelo!
>
> *Duke.* This nor hurts him, nor profits you a jot.
> Forbear it therefore; give your cause to heaven.
> Mark what I say, which you shall find
> By every syllable a faithful verity.

$$(113–26)$$

But in the syllables that follow there is clearly intermixed with truth "deliberate mystification" (Lever). If you are suffering in the injurious world (the Reformers warned) true religion does not urge you to seek for "faithful verity" in the words or authority of man. The Friar would earnestly persuade her to his direction.

> If you can pace your wisdom
> In that good path that I would wish it go,
> And you shall have your bosom on this wretch,
> Grace of the Duke, revenges to your heart,
> And general honour.
>
> *Isab.*   I am directed by you.
>
> (132–36)

Not heavenly grace; not the forgiveness from charity in the heart ("Thou shalt not hate thy brother in thine heart" [Levit. 19:17]); not honor before God. Some patience, some giving of her cause to heaven, some holy Friar. The Duke-Friar concludes detailed orders for her with a paradoxical assurance.

> Command these fretting waters from your eyes
> With a light heart; trust not my holy order,
> If I pervert your course.—Who's here?
>
> (146–48)

Shakespeare, in the writing, may well have gone out for a short one before he answered that question with the intrusion of Lucio for the scene's concluding groupings. For Lucio begins with a howler about the time of day that remained uncorrected, and Shakespeare (as Lever suggests) may have revised here or at least (as I imagine) completed the scene to include Lucio at another sitting.[79] What we have, however, well coheres. Of course Lucio needs to be reintroduced to prepare for his role in the finale by renewing his slander of the Duke and by having his boastful mouth betray him into a confession of his having evaded marriage to the wench he impregnated. But there is more to it than that.

By a typical compression, Lucio already knows of Claudio's death, sympathizes with Isabella for her reddened eyes, counsels patience—and all at once blurts out how his appetite now has him terrified for his own head.

> *Lucio.* O pretty Isabella, I am pale at mine heart to see thine eyes
> so red: thou must be patient.—I am fain to dine and sup with
> water and bran: I dare not for my head fill my belly: one
> fruitful meal would set me to't.—
>
> (150–54)

But he seems genuinely to grieve over Claudio and is sure of one thing, "if the old fantastical duke of dark corners had been at home, he had lived" (156–57). Isabella, still silent, probably should exit at this point, leaving the Duke to retort on his own behalf. But it is a most interesting effect, given the recent exposure of both characters beneath their religious costumes, to have Lucio refer with such grossness to sexual appetite. We have already heard him speak memorably to this point without such elaborated reference to the connection of diet and sex in the Elizabethan physiological theory of love ("it is impossible to extirp it quite, friar, till eating and drinking be put down" III.ii.98–99).[80] Here the faux pas heightens our awareness of the characters who hear him, and presumably these people are not immune to the sexual drive either. The heated exasperation with which the Friar almost in the Duke's voice responds to Lucio's crack about the Duke's sly assignations naturally seems to have something to do with the presence of the lady; and he protests too much besides, for Lucio's sobriquet for the secretive-crafty and benign ruler, less its slanderous sense, is the one everyone finds the most apt in the play for the Duke. What else does Lucio say that has a truth? He persists in pursuing the sensitive point about the Duke's being a good "woodman" and gets a promise for the future to ignore.

> *Duke.* Sir, the Duke is marvellous little beholding to your reports; but the best is, he lives not in them.
>
> *Lucio.* Friar, thou knowest not the Duke so well as I do.
> He's a better woodman than thou tak'st him for.
>
> *Duke.* Well! you'll answer this one day. Fare ye well.
>
> *[going.]*
>
> *Lucio.* Nay, tarry, I'll go along with thee: I can tell thee pretty tales of the Duke.
>
> (158–64)

This reprise of their earlier doubly charged routine renews our sense of the Duke as comically imposed on in his disguise to listen to tales of his flesh-mongering. Twice he tries to walk away from this company, but Lucio is not so easily shaken off and insists on going right along with him.

> *Duke.* Sir, your company is fairer than honest; rest you well.

Lucio. By my troth. I'll go with thee to the lane's end. If bawdy talk
offend you, we'll have very little of it.
Nay, friar, I am kind of burr, I shall stick.   *Exeunt.*

(173–77)

Something more than Lucio sticks like a burr, and that is the
mocking of the disclaimer of being (like the audience) a suitable
audience for bawdy. One reason we enjoy Lucio is that we are
scandal mongers about the great too, and enjoy having them taken
down to our level. And Shakespeare makes us undergo, in the more
considerate experience of the theater, that other elementary truth
about slander, that repeated often enough something of it will ad-
here. Angelo's deeds are appalling in part because they make calumny of the great sound like truth. Slander has its darker side,
necessarily to be addressed by the Duke in his concern for the
very viability of effective authority in the state and society. But in
the course of the laughter raised by the persistence of the self-
justifying male-gossip and spokesman for the lusts of the flesh, the
audience has been subliminally prepared for a central surprise of
the conclusion.

*   *   *

The three brief scenes that lead directly to the finale—the first
set the night before, the second the next morning, the third ending
with the urgent report that the citizens are in place and "the Duke
is ent'ring"—make a hastening sequence that might justly be titled
"The Actors, and the Producer-Director, Prepare." With the performance looming next day, two of the producer's assistants find his
successive missives to them so contradictory they wonder if he
might be mad. And what is this wild card he wants thrown in of
having members of the audience participate if they choose to gripe
about past performances? Well, that at least will deliver these temporary managers of the show from complaints of their performance
hereafter (iv.1–12). Alone, he who has played the chief actor-
manager worries that he is not up for the performance (18–32).
What he has done in his not-indeed-private personal life gives the
lie to his persona: it "unshapes [him] quite"—(a "shape" can be
an actor's costume); it distracts him from the proceedings and
splits his concentration. He could be found out in it, but thinks
the only one who could call him, unlike her brother whose shame

would have made him dangerous, too ashamed of what's been done to challenge him. But his deed does. And the deed—he wishes it were otherwise—is done, irrevocably done, and grace has gone with it. He will just have to go on with the show as he now must play it. It is bound to be a forced, and false, performance.

The Producer-Director, who has also given himself the juiciest and of course the most authoritative part, now appears splendidly dressed for it, ordering proprieties to support it according to the scenario he has in mind. One principal stooge (the Provost) already "knows our purpose and our plot" (v.2). As he gives another property letters to be delivered to him "at fit time" (1) in the performance—(the emphatic point is local; no such letters in fact are used)—he exhorts him to keep to directional instruction and, amidst the inevitably improvisational elements of the performance, always to hold to the scenario-maker's "special drift."

> The matter being afoot, keep your instruction,
> And hold you ever to our special drift,
> Though sometimes you do blench from this to that
> As cause doth minister.
>
> (3–6)

He then posts calls to assure he will come on properly supported with a noble retinue suiting his ducal role and bids these actors "bring the trumpets to the gate" (9) to proclaim the performance, and the theme of fame, before his entry.[81] That is not to be (as in one source it is) a "royal entry" in the grand style complete with Nine Worthies and other flattering and didactic shows declaring the virtues of the ruler and good government. The rattled-off names of his heraldically supporting nobles—one that of a worthy, the others Roman, smacking of civic virtue—must metonymously serve. But one shows up early for his call to be greeted warmly. His name, Varrius, is that of a father of a prototype of princes of dark corners, Alexander Severus.[82]

Finally, with only moments till showtime, the leading lady has an attack of anxiety, and scruples, about her casting, which does not suit her character, so she will really have to play it, and she is loath to speak so indirectly. All these lies, and why? The accuser's role, she says to Mariana, "that is your part" (vi.1–4). Besides, all she has is her "side" and the Director's forewarning (5–8), so she will not think it strange, that in the performance he may speak against her "on the adverse side." But if he does, his comfort in advance is scarcely more assuring; "That's bitter to sweet end" surely sounds hard-to-swallow medicine. But now their prompter, in the person of the Duke-Director's Friar Peter, hastily summons them to take their positions onstage where he has marked "a stand most fit" for their plotted interception of the Duke (10–12). The audience of noble and grave citizens is attentively in place. "Twice have the trumpets sounded" (12–14)—as they did in the public theater before a performance; "The Duke is ent'ring" (15) and off they rush, for the show is about to begin.

* * *

John Masefield, who found *Measure for Measure* "constructed closely and subtly for the stage," thought that "it is more full of the ingenuities of play-writing than any of the plays." He also accurately judged it "a marvellous piece of unflinching thought."[83] No part of the play exhibits these characteristics more distinctly and remarkably than its conclusion. But we are not likely to see the one without the other. What blocks our vision is the one proposition shared by both principal armies of critics entrenched in stalemate over the play, whose catastrophe is the ground of their most sanguinary and dubious battle. On one side are arrayed those indignant at the ending. Deploring or ridiculing its dispositions, they find in them the final proof of Shakespeare's failure in imposing a comic close on an action embarrassed or violated by it—one whose tragic or problematic seriousness cannot bear its religious resolution. Opposed are the fervent ranks of those who celebrate such a resolution as the entirely appropriate Christian ending of a play throughout accordant with the Sermon on the Mount. If "the thought . . . seems strange, or the action unreasonable, it will be found to reflect the sublime strangeness and unreason of Jesus' teaching" (Wilson Knight).[84] The Duke's "total attitude," we are told, is that of the play and plainly is meant by the dramatist to be ours (Leavis). The well-intentioned Ruler who has looked on Angelo's passes like Power Divine, and rescued the situation, returns to bring good out of evil, and the conclusion shaped by his "aptness in remission" is properly the resonant happy ending of Shakespeare's play. Both sides have much to teach us about the play, both where they are right and where they are wrong. However, the central point in which they agree though at loggerheads, is that the Duke essentially is the play's *deus ex machina* and that the ending as he would dictate it must be supposed identical with Shakespeare's conclusion of his play. But the play denies that supposition. To warn us off it in advance of the conclusion is the function of the three scenes preceding the Duke's finale, which proclaim it to be a play within the play.

With *Richard II* Shakespeare had become deeply preoccupied with the implications of politics as performance. In its Deposition Scene he presents the struggle of figures, in roles attained and suffered, to impose their antagonistic interpretations of a political event in the public performance that enacts it. The play's abiding question is in the gulf between ceremony and ritual, between the king's two bodies and the name and actuality of power, between authority and its sanction, between mere fallen man and the role of god on earth, between the actual and the ideal. It is about the infeasibility of the play ever being real in an ideal sense. *Hamlet* hugely fulfills the tragic promise of this central nexus of Shakespearean preoccupations, and *Measure for Measure,* like the preceding "problem" plays, was written in its light. This play is built from its beginning on the idea of imposed roles: roles imposed by God, by nature's gifts, by authority divine and secular, by society and family and our fellow man, by the self-misunderstanding self and the errant will. The action is developed and the big scenes all created by the characters' attempts to impose roles on others; and whatever the admixture of tones or the seriousness of thought, those actions are ironic and deflative. The questioning, testing, and weighing to which the characters in turn are subjected form a sequence climaxed with the Duke.

A great deal has been made, in various guises, and protested too, of the Duke as God figure in this play. That the play sees this matter quite differently from the criticism results from the latter's giving insufficient weight to the fact that other characters are placed in the position of being God figures too. In the structure of the playing, the Duke is the third principal character to be so placed. That sequence overarches the so-called split in the play. With Angelo and Isabella earlier emphasized for dramatic economy, it enjoys a reprise for the conclusion that ends in the Duke's attempt to impose roles on all the characters by his judgments and proffered admonitions. The beneficent power that works to contain

dangerous consequentiality, the figure who ministers to his subjects' growth in self-knowledge, the ruler who would finally manage
the action toward comic resolution is no more free of limitation or
immune to irony than his wearing of his two costumes is unat-
tended by contradiction or the relation of his means and ends by
embarrassment. Though Angelo is awed and humbled that the
Duke has looked upon his passes like power divine, the operative
word is *like,* which asserts a similitude while firmly denying an
identity.[85]

Of course the Duke is largely represented as trying to be the
very model of the good ruler. Shakespeare would not have his
profound irony otherwise. The Duke has not been in control of
what arises from the experiment he initiates with such parabolic
overtones. What the empowered Angelo does when temptation
shows him what he is capable of is his doing. The consequences
of that temptation the Duke can expose, but they are not entirely
the Duke's to prevent or undo. His dictates can reframe the stricture of Angelo's circumstance; they cannot dictate the affirmation
of his being to the comic happiness of man new made within it. A
play within a play often tends to heighten the reality of the characters and the world of the primary action and intensify the reference
to actuality in their representation. When the Duke commandeers
the characters for the performance at his return, the effect of their
bringing the recalcitrance of their vividly incarnated beings to the
conclusion he would impose is to heighten the audience's sense of
the difficulties of resolving the problems of their world, of happily
fulfilling the condition of their being, in a play. Robert Ornstein
has written of the ending:

> The ending of the play is unsatisfactory in that it disappoints our long-
> ing for a more perfect justice than the world affords and because it
> avoids the very moral problems which lend reality and meaning to a
> contrived *novella* fable. The conflict between divine commandment and
> human frailty, between the high ethic of the Gospel and the necessity of
> punitive law, is brushed aside, not resolved. To the final scene Angelo's
> legalistic conception of justice remains valid in the eyes of his fellow
> citizens and even triumphs in Isabella's "mercy."[86]

There is brilliance here, but not in the opening judgment. If the
world does not afford what we are disappointed not to get, what
we wanted from *Measure for Measure* was illusion or wish fulfill-

ment—what a play might give us. Shakespeare's ending subsumes that through the Duke's play and his ending for it. But Shakespeare's ending is the only satisfactory one for *his* play because, by holding up the mirror to nature, it gives us what plays rarely do, a measure we are bound to acknowledge for our measure of reality.

* * *

Complimental greeting at the return of his royal grace lets the Duke perform the broad ironies of insisting on "public thanks / Forerunning more requital" for the goodness he has heard of Angelo's justice (V.i.5–8). Accordant dramatic irony in the deputy's response shows him unwarily set up: "You make my bonds still greater" (9). The Duke makes clear he must: it would be unjust of him to imprison within "covert bosom" Angelo's desert when it deserves fit recording in suitably brazen characters against the "razure of oblivion" (10–14). He tops this with covert irony at his own expense by giving him his hand and staging Escalus at his other to let the subject see a heraldic emblem of majesty with its "good supporters," Justice and Mercy (17–19). That is the cue for Friar Peter to prompt Isabella to stage her melodramatic kneeling appeal to the Duke for ". . . justice! Justice! Justice! Justice!" for a deflowered maid (21–26). The moment is seized by the Duke to show, with what may be the most chilling line in the play, what the situation would be like without his presence.

> *Duke.* Relate your wrongs. In what? By whom? Be brief.
> Here is Lord Angelo shall give you justice.
> Reveal yourself to him.
>
> *Isab.*   O worthy Duke,
> You bid me seek redemption of the devil.
> Hear me yourself:
>
>   (27–31)

The "foul redemption" is recalled, and it is already clear that by the Duke's arrangement his ironic promise of public fame for desertful actions in his absence is to apply to Isabella as well. Suspense is built for her recital by two deflections. First, the need to dispel the dismissive imputation that she is mad is used (*à la* Hamlet) to energize her articulation of Angelo's seeming; and second, Lucio unexpectedly takes her mention of his role as messenger as cue to tell his part of the story. The Duke's old *bête noir* puts in for a role that promises a nemesis to dog the ducal show. The Duke takes his time putting Lucio in his place with promises of his own for the future.

> *Duke.* [*to Lucio.*] You were not bid to speak.
>
> *Lucio.*   No, my good lord,
>   Nor wish'd to hold my peace.
>
> *Duke.*   I wish you now, then;
>   Pray you take note of it;
>   And when you have a business for yourself,
>   Pray heaven you then be perfect.
>
> *Lucio.*   I warrant your honour.
>
> *Duke.* The warrant's for yourself: take heed to't.
>
>   (81–86)

But Lucio proves as irrepressible as incorrigible. In the performance of the Duke's comedy he is the licentious clown who insists on interruptively speaking more than is set down for him. In the performance of Shakespeare's play he therefore the more emphatically speaks to the necessary questions of the play then to be considered. (How clever a turn on the idea of the usefulness of license.)

> *Isab.* This gentleman told somewhat of my tale.
>
> *Lucio.* Right.
>
> *Duke.* It may be right, but you are i'the wrong
>   To speak before your time.—Proceed.
>
>   (87–89)

Isabella's flat-footed disarray, Lucio's self-satisfaction, and the Duke's contained exasperation make a fine comic arrest of the proceeding. So much for amateur theatricals.

The entertainment for us in the first accusation of Angelo is in the ensemble of falsity, the multiplicity of audiences—including one who believes the performance entirely real—but most of all in the fact that both accuser and accused are caught out for what they did not do. He had done that which he should not have done— but it was not with her; and she did not do for her brother what she perhaps should have done. The substitution of the bed-trick is reversed, and she is made to claim in public the very shame and dishonor she had refused, all to get at Angelo, and only to be called a liar for it. One clear truth in her narrative, reserved for last, concerns the promise-breach about her brother's life. Her articulation of the point catches attention, for she does not, as we might expect, stress the death of her brother she and Angelo believe in; it is thus made to register so as to undermine a basic argument of her "mercy" speech later on.

> And I did yield to him. But the next morn betimes,
> His purpose surfeiting, he sends a warrant
> For my poor brother's head.
>
> (104–6)

That was a murderous *deed,* not just an "intent."

Her whole story the Duke ridicules for its unlikelihood but projects its improbability as a sardonic indictment of Angelo. There is no inherent reason, he says,

> That with such vehemency he should pursue
> Faults proper to himself. If he had so offended,
> He would have weigh'd thy brother by himself,
> And not have cut him off. Someone hath set you on:
>
> (112–15)

Disappointed, she would in patience leave to God the ultimate unmasking of evil concealed with royal privilege; but the Duke has her arrested and pursues the mind behind the scandalous practice directed at "him so near us" (117–29). That invites Lucio to play what looks to be an important part, attributing his own calumnies of the Duke to the missing Friar. Friar Peter now speaks up to say that he has heard the royal ear abused. First he asserts flatly that this woman has falsely accused the substitute. Yet his report of the Friar is opposite of Lucio's; but then he returns to the vindication of "this worthy nobleman" from the charge of this woman, promising "Her shall you hear disproved" (163). There is nothing literarily distinguished about this long prelude to Mariana's entrance, and the whole passage must seem negligible unless one does what it is essential to do in the reading: namely, see the silent Angelo at the center of it.

From his one line warning the Duke before her testimony that the sister of the condemned "will speak most bitterly and strange" (38), Angelo is silent for 160 lines (until his brief enquiry about Mariana's accusation before he orders her unveiling). His face must strive to give away nothing, but we hear in this sequence of offered opinion the ups and downs for his hopes of escape, and see he is being played with. Here he is at an upbeat. The witness they are to hear is to clear him of the sister's accusation; but the veiled woman who appears, from what she says even before unveiling, will be identified by the Duke as "no witness for Lord Angelo" (192). Angelo's silence itself is made articulate in the covering speech just preceding the veiled Mariana's entrance before them where the Duke, all confidence in his deputy, calls for seats, offers to be a mere auditor, and tellingly prompts Angelo "be you judge / Of your own cause" (167–69). Angelo does not do that here; the seed is planted for him to request such a power when his patience is touched later. But his preoccupation is registered, because Angelo, in character, would object to the naked injustice of such a proceeding, as the Duke-Friar later does.

The air of mystery the veiled figure brings comes complete with formulaic riddle of her identity; but that is brought down to earth when Lucio gives a pertinently bawdy solution, taking off from the Duke's conclusion that, being neither maid, widow, nor wife, she is "nothing": "My lord, she may be a punk. . ." (178–81). He does the same for the riddle of the unmarried woman with a husband who knows not that ever he knew her as his wife ("He was drunk" [187–89]). Mariana's veil of course declares that her public identity cannot be clarified until her "husband" identify himself by bidding her to remove it. Her unmasking integrates the woman before Angelo with his once contracted, vowed, and handfasted bride and with the body "that took away the match from Isabel" (210). Lucio serves again by sounding a bass part to the Duke's seeming-innocent question for Angelo.

> *Duke.*   Know you this woman?
>
> *Lucio.* Carnally, she says.
>
> *Duke.*   Sirrah, no more!
>
> *Lucio.* Enough, my lord.
>
>   (212–14)

Here starts Angelo's first substantial speech in the scene (215–23). And the cleverness of the speech is that it really does not expose his hypocrisy in the present situation; rather, his hypocrisy in the past situation is brought into the present. In this accusatory sequence, complemental to the first, both accuser and accused are caught out for what they did do—but he thinks he knows he did not. In recounting his old reasons for rejecting her he mendaciously omits the vowed contract, but he really can say with perfect conscience that he has not spoken with her, seen her, heard from her in five years. Her affirmation of the truth of their relation finally angers him to ask the Duke for "the scope of justice"—to be used, to do him credit, to discover the practice of "the mighty member" that sets on "these poor informal women" to abuse him (233–38). The Duke's hearty concurrence and ironic encouragement broaden out into a larger mockery of prejudgment.

> Let me have way, my lord,
> To find this practice out.
>
> *Duke.*   Ay, with my heart;
> And punish them to your height of pleasure.
> Thou foolish friar, and thou pernicious woman,
> Compact with her that's gone: think'st thou thy oaths,
> Though they would swear down each particular saint,
> Were testimonies against his worth and credit,
> That's seal'd in approbation?
>
> (237–44)

This reaches beyond Angelo to question anyone's claim to be authoritatively marked once and for all as tested true to standard. A single temptation can give our "worth" the lie. Indeed, a theological sense may ironically insinuate itself in "seal'd," for sacraments regularly are called "seals" of grace or redeemed sin.[87]

Ordering Escalus to assist in investigating this abuse, the Duke exits to transform himself into the Friar he points to as the one "that set them on" (247). In fact Angelo, after his speech asking with unconscious irony for the scope of justice, remains silent at the margins of the investigation, which approaches the farcical in the hands of Escalus and Lucio. Only after eighty-four lines, in the midst of the examination of the truculently outrageous Friar, does he briefly contribute to what finally becomes Lucio's comic discovery of the Duke beneath the Friar's hood. As the Friar, the

Duke greets their great place with scathing respect, asserts the Duke's injustice in being gone, thus putting the trial of innocents in the mouth of the villain they have come to accuse; and again, as no subject of the Duke but an onlooker, tasks the state—his own state—for so countenancing faults that corruption o'erruns the stew—a pun which, like the reference to "forfeits in a barber shop," wryly tempers the letter-of-the-law severity his criticism champions (290–320). The whole preceding enacted argument about scope and restraint, leniency and severity, is reawakened just as the near-apoplectic Escalus is to order the Friar to the rack and the revelation of the Duke exposes the deposed Angelo to the humbling completeness of his own unmasking.

> *Ang.*   O my dread lord,
> I should be guiltier than my guiltiness
> To think I can be undiscernible,
> When I perceive your Grace, like power divine,
> Hath looked upon my passes. Then, good prince,
> No longer session hold upon my shame,
> But let my trial be mine own confession.
> Immediate sentence, then, and sequent death
> Is all the grace I beg.
>
>   (364–72)

Angelo addresses the secular authority but in such terms as must compel us to see "all the grace" he begs against the expectations of spiritual repentance. Recalling that Juliet took her shame with joy, we are bound to see Angelo in his total humiliation the spokesman for strict justice still. That situation is a very subtle manipulation of the audience in anticipation of the ending. In effect Angelo preempts our desire to see him get what he deserves, but we can hardly indulge that desire and hope for grace to escape our own whipping. The doubtfulness of his repentance already is poised against the audience's unreadiness to forgive, and both are poised against the fact that divine grace is a gift of unmerited mercy.

The Duke's response is only to call Mariana hither and ask Angelo whether he ever was contracted to her, and at his simple admission that he was, to order him offstage with Friar Peter and the Provost to "marry her instantly" and return. While that marriage is taking place offstage, the Duke, beginning with the same "come hither" he had used to Mariana, declares himself to Isabella.

Duke.   Come hither, Isabel.
    Your friar is now your prince. As I was then,
    Advertising and holy to your business,
    Not changing heart with habit, I am still
    Attorney'd at your service.

                                              (379–83)

While the couple offstage is exchanging vows, these two ask each other's pardon. This implicit juxtaposition subtly inflects the entire close-up on the Duke and Isabella, but the effect is assimilated to the subtext guaranteed by the Duke's already *announced* covert involvement in her life. Isabella asks pardon for having "employ'd and pain'd" his "unknown sovereignty," the Duke, addressing her as "dear maid," for having failed to manifest his power in time to save her brother's life. His excuse is to us patently face-saving since it was precisely to premature revelation of his power that he had to resort to save Claudio. As the audience needs no such explanation, it is emphasized that the Duke's relationship with Isabella requires it. His speech softens the earlier impression of insensitivity in manipulating her while in fact priming her for the role planned for her that finally will clarify his purposes in keeping her ignorant of her good.

Duke.   You are pardon'd, Isabel.
    And now, dear maid, be you as free to us.
    Your brother's death, I know, sits at your heart:
    And you may marvel why I obscur'd myself,
    Labouring to save his life, and would not rather
    Make rash remonstrance of my hidden power
    Than let him so be lost. O most kind maid,
    It was the swift celerity of his death,
    Which I did think with slower foot came on,
    That brain'd my purpose. But peace be with him.
    That life is better life, past fearing death,
    Than that which lives to fear. Make it your comfort,
    So happy is your brother.

Enter Angelo, Mariana, *Friar* Peter, [*and*] Provost.

Isab.   I do, my lord.

                                              (385–97)

Critics obviously have better things to talk about, and better poetry to quote, than this prolix speech of lame explanation with embarrassments the order of "swift celerity" and that foot of death that comes so near bashing out the brains of the Duke's purpose. The man who wrote the Pyramus and Thisbe play can be fascinatingly interested in the dramatic use of "bad writing," and here he had good cause to make the Duke's use of his awkward situation serve his own needs. The tireless iteration of "your brother's death" is not so much needed by Isabella, as by the audience that knows his life has been saved. If her kneeling to ask mercy for Angelo, coming shortly, is to have full effect, the audience must have a recently vivified sense of the factuality of his death to her, and what better way than to have this apology for having failed to prevent it? The Duke's emphasis on her relation to Claudio ("O most kind maid") is for Isabella as well as for us, as his later speeches countering Mariana's pleas to her prove. So too, in part, is the implicit reference to Claudio's fear of death upon which she turned her back. But the Duke's conclusion looks out on a theme as important to the ending of the play as it was to its middle—the relation of fitness to die to fitness to live. Lever spoils the Duke's wit in glossing "That life" as Isabella would hear it, "The life to come." For the audience the primary meaning may be the "better life" the living Claudio now is "happy" in, which does not live to fear. These lines of course recall the Duke's crucial speech in III.i and they confirm it was meant to convey an assurance of the Duke's intention to save Claudio. But, brilliantly, it is Angelo, not Claudio, who enters at the words "your brother" before Isabella responds to the Duke with her "I do."

Here is yet another variation in the relating of successive groupings—an interlace. The Duke's first lines, starting "For this new-married man approaching here," serve to cover Angelo and Mariana's approach. They tell Isabella that she "must pardon / For Mariana's sake" Angelo's wrong against her own "well-defended honour" (398–401). By that point, Angelo is placed before him to get both barrels of the Duke's condemnation. The speech builds and builds, through recall of the mercy of the law to biblical echoes of the Law, to the misleading sense, linking it with the *lex talionis,* of the play's title, to the sentencing itself.

We do condemn thee to the very block
Where Claudio stoop'd to death, and with like haste.
Away with him.

(412–14)

It is at this point—not later when Angelo perceives he is safe, as many writers on the play leave us to suppose—that the audience knows the Duke's intention is to save him, and to make the action of the play he dominates into a comedy. This announcement decisively splits the audience onstage, who believe Claudio dead and Angelo condemned to die, from Shakespeare's audience in the theater, the latter being freed to consider all the more objectively the reactions of those onstage to what is now a hypothetical situation, to see what in context that reveals, and to weigh the Duke's promised ending in the light of it.

With the Duke's announcement to the theater audience comes an immediate, if momentary, shift to a comic tone.

Mariana.   O my most gracious lord,
      I hope you will not mock me with a husband.

Duke.   It is your husband mock'd you with a husband.

(414–16)

In the same cool dry manner, he explains in completely worldly terms the fitness of the marriage he ordered, as a measure designed to safeguard her honor and protect her good to come. He adds, almost as an afterthought, that Angelo's possessions though the crown's by confiscation he invests and "widows" her with "To buy you a better husband" (420–23). Here is an icy appraisal indeed of the marriage market and what is considered worth upon it. We cannot choose but think of worthy Angelo's calculated escape from marriage vowed and contracted *de futuro* to desert Mariana because her dowry had been lost at sea. Respects of fortune were his love. The dramatist who was within a year to produce the scene of Cordelia and her suitors wrote this passage, and he gave us first in Mariana a warmly human embodiment of essential worth in a context of valuing where (as he will later write) "Love's not love / When it is mingled with regards that stands / Aloof from th'entire point" (*Lear* I.i.239–40).

Mariana.   O my dear lord,
          I crave no other, nor no better man.

Duke.   Never crave him; we are definitive.

                                                        (423–25)

The word *crave* here is deeply right and Shakespeare by the Duke's repetition immediately stamps it into our memories for later use. Enthusiastic interpretation that tries simply to assimilate Mariana's love to the sublime unreason of Christian teaching betrays the representation. What is "against all sense" in that meaning we are to come to in a moment. Here, quite as irreducible and in its own way as mysterious, is something differently against all sense, and that is human love. The urgency and absoluteness of its commitment assure we will not see it simply as a *donnée* of romance. And the way it is regarded is very different too from the analytic view of love's choice of the unworthy in *Troilus* or even in *All's Well,* for Mariana is not blind to Angelo's badness, and Bertram is no Angelo.

The Duke's adamant refusal to allow her pleas to alter his definitive judgment and then his turning from her to deal with Lucio precipitates Mariana's anguished appeal to Isabella to join her on her knees. In her plea, "—sweet Isabel, take my part" becomes itself a stage direction, a plea for requital of the substitution, and above all a moving attempt to impose a role that tests the willingness and capacity of the character to undertake it. As the focus intensifies with the suspense, there is an operalike effect of externalized articulation for the hesitant and silent Isabella. The voice of the Duke, arguing the dead brother's claims upon her to stand for avenging justice, is set against Mariana's urging of what might be the consequence in the life of the forgiven of Isabella's kneeling down "in mercy of this fact."

Duke.   Against all sense you do importune her.
          Should she kneel down in mercy of this fact,
          Her brother's ghost his paved bed would break,
          And take her hence in horror.

Mariana.   Isabel!
          Sweet Isabel do yet but kneel by me;
          Hold up your hands, say nothing: I'll speak all.
          They say best men are moulded out of faults,

And, for the most, become much more the better
For being a little bad. So may my husband.
O Isabel! Will you not lend a knee?

(431–40)

Here surely may be found reference to "the fortunate fall" that allegorically minded critics are prone to believe so largely proclaimed in the play's conclusion. Isabella is asked to be the forgiving intercessor for fallen man, pleading for mercy before the just ruler who, like power divine, has condemned him as deserving of death. But in Elizabethan religious literature the nearest parallels to Mariana's argument, which has not one specific Christian reference in it, occur in the frequent discussions of the value of divinely permitted temptation, the good for our soul that can come of our falls. That was one of the meanings in Escalus's "Some rise by sin." Mariana speaks of her husband's betterment through his fall in the most human sense that accords with argument and discovery earlier in the play—that actual sense of our own frailty is necessary to our goodness, that it is only when we realize what we should be if judged as we are that mercy then can breathe within our lips *like* man new made.

But that is the key to the surprise achieved by Isabella's words. Mariana's plea to the silently standing Isabel, emphasizing that she begs her but to kneel by her and only mutely implore while she herself speaks, carefully prepares us to see Isabella's gesture and speech separately. Her earlier kneeling performance in the scene, ironically enough for justice, helps make this extempore one for mercy touchingly real and, though levered from her, an act deliberately chosen—as if the compulsion to play the role moves her to see the inner necessity in herself to play it. The spokesperson for the ideal of mercy who had fearfully and vindictively hurled at her brother "Might but my bending down / Reprieve thee from thy fate, it should proceed"—now kneels to implore that her enemy be spared. Her answering to Mariana's need (though it also argues a growth in womanly understanding) and her surrender of vengeful justice for forgiveness make her kneeling an act of Christian mercy that the speeches of Mariana and the Duke have defined in advance. Interpretation cannot be far wrong in finding it such. Where it certainly goes wrong is in supposing, in consequence, that her speech is of Christian mercy all compact with her gesture. She has already done that doctrinal turn, and memorably even if it then cost her nothing, in the first interview with Angelo. That her speech here comes climactically emphasizes how very surprisingly different an utterance it is.

> *Isab.*   [*kneeling.*]   Most bounteous sir:
> Look, if it please you, on this man condemn'd
> As if my brother liv'd. I partly think
> A due sincerity govern'd his deeds
> Till he did look on me. Since it is so,
> Let him not die. My brother had but justice,
> In that he did the thing for which he died:
> For Angelo,
> His act did not o'ertake his bad intent,
> And must be buried but as an intent
> That perish'd by the way. Thoughts are no subjects;
> Intents, but merely thoughts.
>
> *Mariana.*   Merely, my lord.
>
>   (441–52)

In parallel to her earlier kneeling speech, this one mixes the factitious with the truth. What is factitious is the entirely dubious argument basing the plea, surprisingly, on the legal distinction between intent and deed. She is not imploring God to forgive his sin or a Christian ruler to temper justice with mercy, but pleading that the secular authority not condemn Angelo for what he literally did not do. The convoluted and interrupted thought depends on her looking on the condemned man as she asks the Duke to do: "As if my brother liv'd," because her brother was condemned for an act the law deemed worthy of death. But to say her brother "did the thing for which he died" provokes an automatic protestation, for had he died, Claudio would not have perished for what he did but at Angelo's hands, and he would not have had "but justice." Moreover, the first crime for which the Duke has sentenced Angelo is, precisely like Claudio's, "violation of sacred chastity"—and the Duke had to mean Mariana. The bad intent of Angelo which Isabella focuses upon is also what the Duke singled out even before he sentenced Angelo just as the wronging of herself in Angelo's "salt imagination" she must forgive for Mariana's sake. What she, astonishingly, finally argues is that Angelo should not die because his act did not overtake his bad intent to lie with her.

In view of the turpitude Angelo himself thinks worthy of death, that argument is indeed "against all sense" and not in view of the sublime unreason of Jesus' teachings. From beginning to end it therefore concentrates our attention on what compels it. Dr. Johnson scornfully located that in its weakest aspect, as the feminine extenuation of Angelo's crime from which she forms a plea in his favor. He thereby reached the famous judgment commentators have wrestled with from the very year it was published.

From what extenuation of his crime can *Isabel,* who yet supposes her brother dead, form any plea in his favour? *Since he was good 'till he looked on me, let him not die.* I am afraid our Varlet Poet intended to inculcate, that women think ill of nothing that raises the credit of their beauty, and are ready, however virtuous, to pardon any act which they think incited by their own charms.[88]

Johnson projected his own intention to inculcate on the poet; and he traps Isabel's meaning in the grip of his own satiric ridicule of the fair sex and in the iron order of his prose. What he locks out is that she says what the audience knows to be the truth. Of course the speech is strangely self-regarding in its context, and it does disclose her realization of herself as a woman. But it is not out of a vain boast but a sense of her responsibility that she speaks. She is displayed as she discovers herself, however innocent, implicated in the toils of human circumstance from which evil bred, and not aloof from it. In that discovery, and not in Christian doctrine itself, an access to forgiveness is found.

But "our Varlet Poet" is up to something even slier than Johnson appears to have imagined. There are three points. First, Isabella is arguing to save a man another woman loves. Although her intent is surely not to compete with Mariana, her speech fairly shouts, "He wanted me; I was the one he really wanted." And that's true too, and we are not likely to forget it when the Duke twice charges Angelo to love Mariana. Again, the hypothetical idea with which Isabella opens her argument—"As if my brother liv'd"—is not for the audience hypothetical at all. Her extraordinary argument, throughout emphasizing Angelo's intents, actually has the effect of making evident to the audience that (as Dr. Johnson insisted) "Angelo had committed all the crimes charged against him, as far as he could commit them." When Angelo perceives he's safe because Claudio lives, the audience is not likely to forget that either. Angelo himself has assured that. The third point, and the first to be ironically brought home, before the muffled Claudio is brought onstage, is that Angelo is so mindful of his crimes that he entreats the death he deserves and would not willingly desire the mercy that Mariana and Isabella have so dramatically implored.

The Duke himself curtly dismisses their suit as "unprofitable" and sharply orders them off their knees ("Stand up, I say"), leaving the disposition of Angelo suspended as he bethinks himself of "another fault" (453–54). That is the Provost's in having Claudio executed at an unusual hour by authority of a private message and not by "a special warrant for the deed" (455–58). Again, a jab at Angelo's "intention." This turn with the Provost—his discharge from his office, asking pardon, offer as testimony of his repenting obedience to the message, too late to save Claudio, to produce another prisoner, Barnardine, reserved alive "that should by private order else have died" (459–67)—transparently is the rigmarolle prepared with the Duke to achieve with Claudio's appearance the *coup de théâtre* of the Duke's play. While the Provost is off to effect this, a brief grouping focused on Angelo is interposed to link the pleas for him with what is immediately to come at the reentry of the Provost.

> [*Exit* Provost.]
>
> *Esc.* I am sorry one so learned and so wise
>   As you, Lord Angelo, have still appear'd,
>   Should slip so grossly, both in the heat of blood
>   And lack of temper'd judgement afterward.
>
> *Ang.* I am sorry that such sorrow I procure,
>   And so deep sticks it in my penitent heart
>   That I crave death more willingly than mercy;
>   'Tis my deserving, and I do entreat it.
>
> *Enter* Provost *with* Barnardine, Claudio, [*muffled, and*] Juliet.
> (468–75)

"I am sorry" is the theme for two voices, two judges. Angelo clearly is deeply remorseful and contrite; but that does not suffice for repentance. That a character announces himself as "penitent" does not make him so (as some readers seem to suppose); in this play it makes us look to see if he is, and what follows to Barnardine confirms the propriety of doing so. Earlier, death was all the grace Angelo begged of the Duke; here he craves death more willingly than mercy, and the same suggestion of spiritual inadequacy in that stance remains. But there is no Friar here to try his "penitence, if it be sound, / Or hollowly put on" (II.iii.22–23). We cannot know. The spiritual delimitation he demonstrates is in looking only at his earthly situation as judge of his own cause. But the previous context, including the speech of his former fellow judge to which he responds, invites him and us to do just that. The "mercy" he refers to is that that the women have implored; and his craving death most ironically recalls Mariana's craving him for her husband. Of course the audience, situated on earth too, agrees with Angelo, who is tolerable because his judgment coincides with what it thinks he deserves. But that (as we have seen) is a trap, because we should know better. Angelo's view here is consistent with his earlier commitment to a narrowly rigid conception of justice, and he demonstrates delimitation even as judge of his earthly circumstance. Escalus's last line—"And lack of temper'd judgement afterward"—is weakly referenced to the perfidy against Claudio so it can register more largely here. Angelo craves for himself a judgment made in ignorance of a central fact which a judge acting with properly "temper'd judgement" would have to know. The chief judge standing silent through this grouping, and very much part of it by his mere presence, does know that fact, as in a moment the stage audience will know it as well as the theater audience has known it.

With Barnardine standing before the Duke, and the muffled Claudio onstage, a fresh triumvirate of characters is illuminated in imagination because of their views of death. Angelo craves it, Barnardine is quite indifferent, and Claudio, once so terrified of it and though still a blindfolded prisoner, has been better advised. But the Duke is talking about life and according to what apprehension of existence it should be squared, and all three have been worldlings. In criticism of the play's concluding judgments Barnardine rarely is given the central prominence and pride of place that Shakespeare confers on him.

Duke. Which is that Barnardine?
Prov. This, my lord.

Duke. There was a friar told me of this man.
Sirrah, thou art said to have a stubborn soul
That apprehends no further than this world,
And squar'st thy life according. Thou'rt condemn'd;
But, for those earthly faults, I quit them all,
And pray thee take this mercy to provide
For better times to come. Friar, advise him;
I leave him to your hand.

(476–84)

Here is the longest speech used for any of the judgments, introducing them by dealing with the limiting case. Barnardine's being told of the limits of his apprehension before being pardoned illuminates the removal of Claudio's blindfold, which Lever says is of that love "whose view is muffled still" (*Romeo* I.i.176). The murderer and the sexual offender, the thief who falsely takes away a life true made and the counterfeiter who puts mettle in restrained means to make a false one, a final time are brought together for judgment onstage. And both reflect Angelo. Since Barnardine has actually taken a life, earning the kindly Provost's unwillingness to pity him "though he were my brother," it is all the harder for an audience to object to the sparing of Angelo. As Barnardine has reflected us, and yet does, we are addressed by the tolerance that would give him the mercy we would want "to provide for better times to come." But the Duke can only pray him so to use this mercy; he cannot control the outcome. Shakespeare could too obviously have exploded all the Duke's benign purposes by bringing Barnardine on drunk, and even barring that there are temptations for performance to be abjured. It suffices that this is the character about whom that trustworthy observer the Provost, fed up, has cause to ask rhetorically, "Who can do good on him?" (IV.ii.66) We will hardly forget the Duke's learning by experience the truth of the Provost's warning that as for spiritual advice for Barnardine, "He will hear none." That is his character, dramaturgically by constitution, and given what he stands for our pity might be reserved for Friar Peter, for we obviously should not hold our breath in anticipation of Barnardine's conversion. But the Duke's effort reaches toward that proposal of generous comedy that the comically inflexible character become human—and also escape tragic inflexibility, the propensity of character "not to be other than one thing" (*Cor.* IV. vii.42) to his ruin. Barnardine, in the Duke's hope, is sentenced to a human life he has been denying. However, with all the foregoing, Barnardine's silence is voluble with uncertainty, and that sense of what silence might speak, once in place, is sure to inform the crucial silences following. For from the point that the Provost unmuffles Claudio no one onstage but the Duke speaks—with the exception of Lucio; and when he is squelched, the Duke alone is left to articulate the close. The play's concluding sequence is divided into those three parts.

In the first, the silences are for various astonishments.

> —What muffl'd fellow's that?
>
> *Prov.* This is another prisoner that I sav'd,
> Who should have died when Claudio lost his head;
> As like almost to Claudio as himself. [*Unmuffles Claudio.*]
>
> *Duke.* [*to Isab.*] If he be like your brother, for his sake
> Is he pardon'd; and for your lovely sake
> Give me your hand and say you will be mine[,]
> He is my brother too: but fitter time for that.
> By this Lord Angelo perceives he's safe;
> Methinks I see a quickening in his eye.
> Well, Angelo, your evil quits you well.
> Look that you love your wife; her worth, worth yours.
>
> (484–95)

Here a major advantage conferred by Claudio and Isabella's silent reconciliation in III.i becomes apparent. Kenneth Muir admired their silent reunion here as a little-recognized masterstroke.[89] But the performer of the gratitude, wonder, and joy Johnson thought strangely missing from the text has to be jot-quick about it because the Duke immediately claims her attention for the yet bigger astonishment that quite surprises the audience as well. "Give me your hand" does not require responsive gesture from Isabel. The thought is conditional (and the Arden's period after "mine" an error): "and for your lovely sake [, if you] give me your hand and say you will be mine, / He is my brother too." The focus remains on the Duke, moreover, because quite as startling for the audience as the proffered proposal is the fact that he comes as close here as he does (especially in the speaking) to making himself symmetrical with Angelo by asking the gift of her chastity for the saving of her brother's life.[90] At this point the temptation of the critic is to conflate this reference to the proposal with his later one and ponder its dramatic propriety, Isabel's reaction (which here needs simply be astonishment), and the significance of the marriage proposed. "But fitter time for that" as the Duke says, directing our attention to create the context that makes us think what Shakespeare would have us think about.

At bottom that is, first of all, structured by symmetry with the relations established early in the play: the Duke paralleled with Angelo, the Duke with Isabella (in the monastery-convent cross-cut), and Isabella with Angelo. To assure this basis of apprehension is the apparent reason Claudio and Juliet are not addressed at all here, although the "quickening in his eye" surely connects with the removal of Claudio's blindfold, just as the denoted recovery of life, or revival, relates to that proposed for Barnardine—but most of all, because of the control of immediate context, to the proposal for Isabella. A most subtle reticence, partly in support of this parallelism, is the Duke's leaving the matter of Angelo's pardon implicit whereas the pardons of Barnardine and Claudio are explicit. Isabella needs no ducal pardon; but, still in the costume of her proposed conventual commitment, she does need enfranchisement "to recover life" (*OED*, v.6). As for Angelo, there is wry observation of the good return for evil that makes his fall so fortunate, and admonition how to be equal to it. "Her worth, worth yours" is densely fused expression referring first to that matter of the lost dowry. Her intrinsic worth makes the match appropriate to your social standing. But also (I think), your worth is to be measured by your properly valuing hers. The straight-eyed admonishment preceding has told Angelo how: "Look that you love your wife." The Duke will think it needful to return to this point in his closing speech, and so will we.

Throughout this passage the Duke speaks in the first person and he will continue to do so until late in his exchange with Lucio. There is cause to notice that in the lightening shift to his self-satisfaction at the "apt remission"—the aptness to pardon offenses—"I find . . . in myself"; for that is calculated to emphasize, as he surveys the company, the exception ("And yet here's one in place I cannot pardon. / [*To Lucio*] You, sirrah . . ."); and Lucio's unpardonable offense is expressed as the unmerited personal injury suffered from the way he extols "me" (496–501). Kirsch of course is right that the Duke clearly is teasing Lucio in adding hanging to the whipping which Lucio proposes as his punishment.

Why some readers should begrudge the Duke, who has comically suffered as butt at Lucio's hands, his getting some of his own back is hard to understand, especially since he again becomes funny by descending to do it. Vengeance and forgiveness, offense and pardon are looked at in a lighter comic vein, but no less pertinently for that, and in fact quite sharply. The Duke's playing with Lucio parodies what he has done with Angelo. And his speech to Lucio on his plans for him is so expressed as to glance at both Angelo (who wronged a woman) and Claudio (who got one with child) and also at the nuptial and execution first proposed as Angelo's sentence. This is reprise.

> *Lucio.* Faith, my lord, I spoke it according to the trick: if you will
>   hang me for it, you may: but I had rather it would please you
>   I might be whipped.
>
> *Duke.* Whipp'd first, sir, and hang'd after.
>   Proclaim it, Provost, round about the city,
>   If any woman wrong'd by this lewd fellow,
>   —As I have heard him swear himself there's one
>   Whom he begot with child—let her appear,
>   And he shall marry her. The nuptial finish'd,
>   Let him be whipp'd and hang'd.
>
> *Lucio.* I beseech your Highness, do not marry me to a whore. Your
>   Highness said even now, I made you a duke; good my lord,
>   do not recompense me in making me a cuckold.
>
> (502–15)

The Duke never refers to the woman Lucio has wronged as a whore; it is left to the sensitivities of the gentleman to make that distinction. That some readers have thought the Duke excessively cruel to Lucio in making him marry a whore, in sentencing him to a living hell as the Elizabethans saw it, is in one sense as disturbing as puzzling. Lucio has wronged a woman. Whether marrying her rights that wrong or truly is a proper "forfeit" of course is another story. Shakespeare is deeply interested in proper bonds as requisite to true freedom, but the Duke has been freeing character after character from imprisonment, and now explicitly sends Lucio to prison. Lucio's voluble, comically exposed, for once really panicked pleas and protests at the life sentence the Duke has decreed voices objection, at a most curious point in a comedy, to marriage *per se* as comic solution. And there are one, or two, other characters onstage who also might similarly object. But Lucio is the very figure of irresponsible man—and it is high time, socially necessary, and only fair that he should be made to endure the bonds, risks, and pain the married men in the audience have to endure. But the point clearly played out in this interposed deflative comedy is that marriage, understood to be a lifetime commitment, is (or can be) a punishment.

> *Duke.*   Upon mine honour, thou shalt marry her.
>   Thy slanders I forgive, and therewithal
>   Remit thy other forfeits.—Take him to prison,
>   And see our pleasure herein executed.
>
> *Lucio.* Marrying a punk, my Lord, is pressing to death,
>   Whipping, and hanging.
>
> *Duke.*   Slandering a prince deserves it.
>
> (516–21)

The Duke's "aptness in remission" also is exposed. Not only King James but Jacobeans of every station would have agreed about the seriousness of slandering a prince; this prince has throughout been preoccupied with the problem, and a crucial aspect of Angelo's corruption is that it defames and vitiates true authority. But that marrying a whore is the punishment that fits the crime surely is hilarious. The dramatic emphasis, moreover, is not on the Blatant Beast, but on the Duke's forgetting his own act of forgiveness but a moment before: "Thy slanders I forgive." He had moved to the royal pronoun to order "our pleasure" that is to be executed, but "Slandering a prince deserves it" is very human. Like Isabella's remarkable plea for mercy, this key moment brings human forgiveness down where we can surely recognize it. And the recognition here is ours, not the Duke's.

The Folio indicates no exit for Lucio at this point, but there must be one. The processional exit at the end otherwise must be as Lever describes, "with Lucio under guard bringing up the rear." But that would be like bringing Barnardine on drunk, much too broad and indiscriminately destructive a comic exposure of the Duke's comedy.[91] Shakespeare's confidence in more subtly communicating the sophisticated balance of his ending is revealed by his ordering Lucio's exit in the text. "Take him to prison, / And see our pleasure herein executed" is not an order to ignore. Lucio's last protest is said over the shoulder as he is being taken off, and the Duke's rejoinder is a fine parting shot. But if Lucio were left onstage, it would never suffice to shut him up. Silence must speak for him now, and it is the silence of those he has analogized. As he gave voice, in his voice and situation to be sure, to something unvoiced in the silence of others, their silence now becomes the more expressive along the lines of his protest.

It is sometimes argued by the Duke-doubters that he has "by his orgy of clemency" undone everything accomplished by the reform administration he empowered.[92] But the brothel-folk and even that frequenter, "light" Lucio, all are in prison and the Duke has before him for the final speech only those he would kindly encourage and direct in the happiness he has formulated for them, those he would thank and promise reward or advancement, and one in both these categories, summing all, to whom he would offer himself in love. The opening lines address the first group and enforce a contrast between the two couples.

> She, Claudio, that you wrong'd, look you restore.
> Joy to you, Mariana; love her, Angelo;
> I have confess'd her, and I know her virtue.
>
> (522–24)

The Duke's firm admonition to Claudio, with Juliet at his side, is one his own desired happiness dictates and no words are needed to express his compliance. But this is the second time the Duke has told Angelo to love Mariana, a necessary persuasion if his wished joy to her is to be fulfilled, and this repetition addresses the second of the objections Angelo had used to justify breaking off the match. First, the Duke had emphasized her worth, and now her virtue. That he should violate the oath about the sanctity of the confessional he never swore implicitly discloses not only the secular ruler (and his presuming an authority not properly his), but an argumentative need of such decisive testimony to be produced. The Duke's extraordinary disclosure calls attention to itself in a way that reminds us of disguise and falsehood in a role at the very point he is urging Angelo to play his imposed role of husband genuinely. Angelo may be silent about these imperatives to love, but Shakespeare's critics are not. Hawkins justly protests that you can't *tell* someone to love another, though she is mistaken to assume that Shakespeare expects us to believe the Duke successfully can for the sake of the play's comic ending. There is another respect in which her position is less than understanding. In fact every man who was properly married in Shakespeare's England was told to love his wife; it is the first duty a husband is ordered to in the Book of Common Prayer, of course following St. Paul. To do the Duke right, he plainly does not suppose his order automatically efficacious. Otherwise he would be fit for such mockery as Hotspur inflicts on Glendower for claiming he "can call spirits from the vasty deep."

> Why, so can I, or so can any man;
> But will they come when you do call for them?
>
> (*1 Hen. IV*, III.i.52–54)

The problem so uniquely presented in Angelo's case is a much more general one than it has appeared. Marriage is the remedy for incontinence and the divinely appointed proper use of potency. Angelo wants to live, pardoned, but his pardon is inseparable from living with a wife he does not love. That "Shakespeare says nothing about the spirit in which Angelo enters this union"[93] is not true. Indeed, even to say (with Hawkins)[94] that there is no evidence that he ever loved her or loves her now is to put the matter the wrong way. Shakespeare has been at pains to show that he did not love her, not only in the story of his cruel abandonment, but more vividly in the admission that until he looked on Isabel he had never experienced "love." In this very scene Angelo has shown he does not love Mariana now by his coldly denying her before her face at a point, ironically, where he feels confident he does not have to be a present hypocrite, only the hypocrite he had been when he broke off the match five years before. The import of the constraint on Angelo's recovered life for the conclusion is enlarged by what follows the Duke's warm expressions of gratitude to Escalus and the Provost. He tells Angelo to pardon the Provost for bringing him Ragozine's head—the offence, he says, pardons itself. But singling out *that* offence leaves dealing with others exposedly finessed. He does not tell Angelo to beg pardon of Claudio or Claudio to forgive him. And they are silent. The hopes for spiritual reconciliation and human fulfillment in new life are most emphatically placed in the relation of the male characters to their mates in marriage.

The key, if penultimate point, then, is the Duke's return to his projected proposal to "Dear Isabel," and enough time has elapsed for Isabel and the audience to entertain it with rather more composure than when startled by the Duke's awkwardly timed introduction of it before.

> Dear Isabel,
> I have a motion much imports your good;
> Whereto if you'll a willing ear incline,
> What's mine is yours, and what is yours is mine.
>
> (531–34)

A point of departure in the genesis of this proposal may be found in the King's matchmaking at the if-ridden ending of *All's Well*, but here the royal figure puts in for himself. The basic impetus of course comes from the conventional requirements of romantic comedy itself. Though much of the play has pivoted on Claudio's fate, he is not its comic hero; and he and Juliet (whether or not she is still big with child[95]) would make, despite the mutuality of their love, a most unsuitably awkward yet-to-be-married pair to be suddenly promoted at center stage as the couple in whom our hopes for comic happiness are projected. In fact their union is upstaged by Angelo's more problematic one. There is no problem for the Duke in his play; Bottom-like, in presuming upon the role of romantic lover to Isabel, he has cast himself as the romantic lead too. Neither is there for Shakespeare in his play any problem he has not deliberately undertaken. It is a wonderful and wildly daring idea, not casually to be attempted, to produce at the very end of a comedy a pair of characters not implausibly offered to fill this great hole in the conventional design whom the audience and the heroine herself had not thought of as a couple at all. Managing the splendid idea of *Much Ado*—to have the audience know better than the ostensible design or the brilliant characters themselves that they are meant for each other and for the comedy's hero and heroine—was simple compared to this, and of course more ingratiating. Here we have suddenly to cast our minds back for hints of the comic action in which they have been blocked as the romantic couple from the fulfillment of themselves and the play in their marriage. Of a case like this to say with Gelb that there is no specific preparation raising expectation of this particular match, and that it therefore fulfills no expectations,[96] is to smother the baby before it breathes.

There have been various sorts of preparation. As we have seen, there are a few groupings with subliminal suggestions, through subtleties of circumstance or some level of the Duke's performance, of a romantic possibility in the relationship. But first of all there is the early parallelism of the two characters in those paired monastic scenes as deniers of love. Miles, considering the tradition, observes that "other disguised dukes show a consistent involvement with love-intrigues."[97] With an open duplicity characteristic of this play, Shakespeare has his Duke Vincentio at once distinguish himself from that conventional expectation by the protest about his "complete bosom" and different motive; but his "Think not" in fact makes us think that protest, in comedy, promises that his bosom will prove indeed to be vulnerable to the "dart of love" (I.iii.1–6). In the scene following, Isabella makes protestation too. Since in these paired scenes with religious setting the first character wants to put on a religious disguise, both Isabella's dialogue with Francisca and the very fact that she is wearing a religious costume but as postulant is not yet sworn to that vocation make us very conscious of the woman who is not yet indeed what her costume would show. When she finally is seen paired with the Duke-Friar in their religious costumes in III.i, in the context of his recruitment of her to participate in effecting his "remedy," an audience prepared by Protestant prejudice about the conventual, the regular clergy, and their relation to nuns is assumed. In *All's Well,* when Lavache claims to have discovered an answer that will fit all questions at court, and the Countess challenges whether it will well fit all, the saucy fool responds:

> As fit as ten groats is for the hand of an attorney, as your French crown for your taffety punk, as Tib's rush for Tom's forefinger, as a pancake for Shrove Tuesday, a morris for May-day, as the nail to his hole, the cuckhold to his horn, as a scolding quean to a wrangling knave, as the nun's lip to the friar's mouth, nay, as the pudding to his skin.
>
> (II.ii.20–27)

Even more important is the development of both characters, particularly Isabella, toward such an end as the Duke wishes to propose. There is no point in exhibiting a self-ignorantly humorless character, immaturely zealous for repressive regulation and unconsciously betraying the self-idealizing fragile sublimation of her passionate nature, if she is not to be brought gradually to self-awareness. The first invitation to her to put on the destined livery of a woman, however outrageously improper itself, makes its point about her and about life, and calls for an appropriate counterpoise in the action. The relationship with Mariana into which she is drawn has the effect, and at points the mystery, of initiation. One value of the nature of the argument given her for her plea for mercy to Angelo is that it shows a woman who well might now consider being called to a vocation other than in a sisterhood of nuns. But we do not know if she knows that yet. Both characters in the proposed couple are destined, and forced by the action, to return from retirement to the world. And "to go to the world" (Beatrice and Lavache remind us) is Elizabethan for "to get married," which is the state of being discussed in the religious literature as that most involved with worldly concerns. But Isabella at the end of the play is still wearing the conventual costume which was treated as a virtual disguise from her first appearance. Here Shakespeare fascinatingly takes off from his treatment of Viola's disguise at the end of *Twelfth Night*. She is, according to the final lines, to be "Orsino's mistress and his fancy's queen" when she has "other habits" than Cesario's to wear. But her "maid's garments" have been legalistically impounded, as it were, along with the Captain at suit of the angry killjoy, who is yet to be entreated to a peace. An offered quickening that "much imports her good" invites Isabel. But whether she has come to such terms within herself about the legalistic killjoy her "disguise" represents as now to put on the destined livery, her silence does not say nor does the text otherwise betray. To have her scorn the Duke's offer to propose to her, as Hawkins mockingly suggests in pique at sentimental effusions over the radiantly smiling acceptance of the Duke imagined by others for Isabel, has been tried in performance (by Jonathan Miller) and it was a predictable disaster. In fact the character is not called upon to show now, in public, whether she wishes to incline a willing ear to the motion the Duke wants to make, and she must not. As she and the Duke, not hand in hand, lead the processional exit at the play's close, her face must be unreadable.

There is preparation of yet another sort for their marriage in the symbolic schema implicit through the analogies of the play.

Christian and other symbolic interpreters of the play since Wilson Knight are not wild-eyed in getting millennial thoughts near the close or in conceiving suggestion in the to-be-proposed marriage of the Duke and Isabella of the union of Mercy and Justice or the spousal of *Sponsus* and *Sponsa*—a consummation devoutly to be wished that every marriage, including Angelo's, was supposed to mirror.[98] But we must know in our hearts from our provoked resentment of the pardon of Angelo, how far we are from the forgiveness and mercy of the Sermon on the Mount. That is to say we have cause to doubt, while we yet do not know, whether the *Sponsa* (the Church and the individual soul) is going to say yes. But if the Duke's success in the action's final attempt to get the heroine to play a role is unknown, there is a hopeful difference between this proposed union and the other marriages. Isabella more distinctly has a choice. That fact illuminates such choice, however heavily encumbered, the others have, down to the very last one in the procession, Barnardine. And it could apply to us too. All the movements expected of romantic comedy—toward both freedom and restoration of legitimate authority, toward a sense of renewed community, toward a wedding of nature and sanctified social art, toward the happiness of lovers in which human fulfillment and continuance are figured—all these have been profoundly qualified by the end of this play. But if comedy in its very essence celebrates human continuance, there is no reason why it may not do so most wryly in realistic view of our best hopes against our imperfection, the limitations of ourselves and our circumstance, the paradoxical nature of our mingled virtues and vices, the ill match of our nature and what is expected of us. It is a very sophisticated catharsis for us to be able to smile at the fact that we are all poor fellows who would live, that the mercy we would ask or offer most often is bawdlike to our vices, and that the vital continuation we so urgently desire may only be the punishment we hope befalls us. "Thou seest, thou wicked varlet now, what's come upon thee. Thou art to continue now, thou varlet, thou art to continue."

As for the royal Bridegroom-in-hope, he says as well of himself, of his union to be proposed, of the procession, of the play's ending, and even of us: "So bring us to our palace." What follows to conclude the play is equally loaded and so striking as to make it puzzling that commentators have virtually ignored it.[99] We are used at the end of Shakespearean comedies to have promise of explanation and exchange of stories. This royal figure, and therefore figure of God on earth, promises something very different.

> So bring us to our palace, where we'll show
> What's yet behind that's meet you all should know.
>> [*Exeunt omnes.*]
>>> (535–36)

What's "behind" is what is yet to come. The playwright's control of the audience's thinking about things to come is always a nice enterprise at the end of a comedy, or indeed any sort of play, and Shakespeare is a close and subtle practitioner in the possibilities of this crucial aspect of his art: where the audience is about to be disengaged from his shaping hands, when the play is over and their immediate future after it becomes their present. That the Duke, in paradigmatically dealing with Barnardine, has prayed him to use "this mercy" he has given him "to provide / For better times to come" has compelled the audience to consider the future of the clement, but demanding, ending he has contrived and to focus on the likelihood of these subjects' using the lives he has reordered for them to so happy an end. If we have been given strong reasons to be skeptical, that is bound to put us in conflict with our proper hope that the Maker of the Comedy will in the end manifestly produce a happy ending out of our stubborn insufficiencies. By acknowledging God's part and by his exhortations, the Duke admitted that he cannot produce it. But here he once more assumes the mystique of secular majesty by which it compliments itself by allowing a pretense to identity with the Providence instrumented by beneficent rule. His usage of "behind" planted ten lines before is quite different from that in the last one:

> Thanks, good friend Escalus, for thy much goodness;
> There's more behind that is more gratulate.
>> (525–26)

The concluding usage is inclusive, not restrictive. Ever the secret plotter, the Duke is going to show them just so much of what is to follow as he deems suitable for them to know. And we will not even be shown that. The actors by their show have shown us all that we are like to know.

And we already have been shown that the Duke is very far from

being omniscient and badly needs the accident that heaven provides to cope with what he has not foreseen. (That may be the
most brilliantly contrived use of accident in comic plotting in all
comedy.) The double identity he has tried—and that, however dis-
tantly and delicately, must ultimately have reference to the English
monarch's being head of church and state—throughout has been
problematic. Temporal power in religious disguise makes religion
"a temporary meddler" (147), and the craft of policy in expedient
practice warps religion from its truth. The conclusion the Duke
benignly has contrived by virtue of his dual role must wait upon
the truly foresightful plans of a far greater inclusive power for
its outcome. The Duke's gracious condescension, in promising to
disclose at his palace what in his judgment is meet for all to know
of what is to come, means that we get to know about what's to
follow for those in the play exactly what that greater power has
deemed it fitting that man know about the future. And that—however many in our artificially illuminated times would presume or
pretend otherwise—is (apart from our deaths) precisely nothing.
That irremoveable fact puts us in our place to know ourselves as
definitively as death or the beams in our eyes when we would judge
others. These last lines provide for the Duke a final suave note of
dry wit and for Shakespeare, ironically twisting their two plays
finally into one, a just ending for his play. His unique entertainment
has with most humane tolerance and profoundly urbane wit mir-
rored for us our nature and condition in the terrestrial city.[100] After
a conclusion that has so notably featured meaning in silence, when
the play's live utterance is ended and the audience otherwise re-
sumes its earthly life, it is entirely appropriate that the rest,
"What's yet behind," should be silence.

Notes

1. Ernest Schanzer, *The Problem Plays of Shakespeare: A Study of "Julius Caesar," "Measure for Measure," "Antony and Cleopatra"* (New York: Schocken, 1963), 71.

2. Roy W. Battenhouse, "*Measure for Measure* and the Christian Doctrine of the Atonement," *Publications of the Modern Language Association* 61 (1946): 1029–59; Una Ellis-Fermor, *The Jacobean Drama: An Interpretation,* 2d ed. rev. (London: Methuen, 1947), 260.

3. A. P. Rossiter, *Angel with Horns: Fifteen Lectures on Shakespeare,* ed. Graham Storey (London: Longmans, 1961), 162. Darryl J. Gless, "*Measure for Measure," the Law and the Convent* (Princeton: Princeton University Press, 1979), 211, more solemnly speaks of "her decision to abandon the rule of St. Clare and marry the Duke."

4. F. R. Leavis, "The Greatness of *Measure for Measure*," *Scrutiny* 10 (1942): 234–47.

5. That is not to deny that the ideas in Guarini's *Compendia della Poesia Tragicomica* (1602), which certainly were in the air, may well have influenced Shakespeare in the formulation of his own practices. See J. W. Lever, ed., *Measure for Measure,* the Arden Shakespeare (London: Methuen, 1967), lxi–lxii (henceforth cited as Lever, ed., *Measure*); also Arthur Kirsch, "The Integrity of *Measure for Measure*," *Shakespeare Survey* 28 (1975): 89–105.

6. See G. K. Hunter, ed., *All's Well that Ends Well,* the Arden Shakespeare (London: Methuen, 1958), 1v.

7. Harriet Hawkins, *Likenesses of Truth in Elizabethan and Restoration Drama* (Oxford: Clarendon Press, 1972), 57–60. Cf. Phillip Edwards, *Shakespeare and the Confines of Art* (London: Methuen, 1968), 119.

8. I think there are good reasons for supposing that *All's Well* preceded *Measure,* but we do not have the evidence to be sure of their relative positions in the chronology. A recent study of the play, David Haley, *Shakespeare's Courtly Mirror: Reflexivity and Prudence in "All's Well that Ends Well"* (Newark: University of Delaware Press; London and Toronto: Associated University Presses, 1993), 254–57, makes a case for dating *All's Well* to 1599, which seems to me too early.

9. See Frederick Sternfeld, "*Troilus and Cressida*: Music for the Play," in *English Institute Essays 1952,* ed. Alan S. Downer (New York: Columbia University Press, 1954), 107–37.

10. Ann Barton, in *The Riverside Shakespeare,* ed. G. Blakemore Evans (Boston: Houghton Mifflin, 1974), 502.

11. Hal Gelb, "Duke Vincentio and the Illusion of Comedy or All's Not Well that Ends Well," *Shakespeare Quarterly* 22 (1971): 32.

12. Meredith Skura, who invokes "a psychoanalytic reading" of the play in "New Interpretations for Interpretation," *Boundary 2* (1979): 50–51, emphasizes the mysterious character of this specified imagined setting for what she finds "at the heart of this play": "an act of sex which is nothing but deception" showing sexual intercourse, like death, to be "a great disguiser." (But on Shakespeare's

unquestionable interest in this, cf. *All's Well* IV.iv.21–25.) The implication of Isabella and the Duke in that "act"—namely, what the play actually *enacts,* this interpreter does not address. Another part of the truth about the locked and barred garden Gless tells us in naming it an enclosed pleasure garden (*Law and the Convent,* 95). It is another *hortus conclusus* ironically to counterpoise the one pointed in the Convent Scene (I.iv) by use of Lucio. See below, n. 39.

13. Northrop Frye, *A Natural Perspective: The Development of Shakespearean Comedy and Romance* (New York: Columbia University Press, 1965), 64.

14. Herbert S. Weil Jr., Rev. of D. L. Stevenson, *The Achievement of Shakespeare's "Measure for Measure,"* 1966, *Shakespeare Studies* 3 (1967): 325. Shakespeare's provision for a reconciliation here was first proposed by Mary Lascelles, *Shakespeare's "Measure of Measure"* (London: Athlone Press, 1953), 90–91, and developed by Lever, ed., *Measure,* xxvi, lxxxii. In a very usefully performance-oriented discussion of the play, Marvin Rosenberg, "Shakespeare's Fantastic Trick: *Measure for Measure,*" *Studies in the Renaissance* 80 (1972): 51–72, unknowingly assumes there has been no reconciliation when he entertains how the characters are to react when Isabel and the revealed Claudio silently confront each other. "If forgiveness is involved, who asks it? Who gives it? Who was judged, who judges? Claudio may very well cut her dead" (70). But that is what Shakespeare is avoiding by preventing.

15. Hawkins, *Likenesses of Truth,* 75.

16. Ibid., 57. But in the very same year Herbert Weil Jr., "Form and Contexts in *Measure for Measure,*" *Critical Quarterly* 12 (1970): 55–72, argued that "Shakespeare again and again calls our attention to the disparity between emotional involvement with his action and the facile formulation that seems inherent in comedy. It is clear that *Measure for Measure* is no attempt at tragedy or melodrama" (70).

17. Bertrand Evans, *Shakespeare's Comedies* (Oxford: Clarendon Press, 1960), 188.

18. George Whetstone, *The Historie of Promos and Cassandra* (London, 1578), 2.1, in Lever, ed., *Measure,* 171. See Geoffrey Bullough, ed., *Narrative and Dramatic Sources of Shakespeare,* vol. 2 of *The Comedies 1597–1603* (London: Routledge and Kegan Paul; New York: Columbia University Press, 1958).

19. Anthony Caputi, "Scenic Design in *Measure for Measure*" (1962), in *Twentieth Century Interpretations of "Measure for Measure,"* ed. George L. Geckle (Englewood Cliffs, N.J.: Prentice-Hall, 1970), 95.

20. David Lloyd Stevenson, *The Achievement of Shakespeare's "Measure for Measure"* (Ithaca: Cornell University Press, 1966), 14.

21. *John Philip Kemble Promptbooks,* ed. Charles H. Shattuck, Folger Facsimiles: Promptbooks Series 1, 11 vols. (Charlottesville: University Press of Virginia, 1974), vol. 6.

22. E. M. W. Tillyard, *Shakespeare's Problem Plays* (London: Chatto and Windus, 1950), 126.

23. Rossiter, *Angel with Horns,* 156–57. In *Troilus and Cressida* (V.ii.140: "If sanctimony be the gods' delight") the word has its earlier, positive sense. The usage in *Measure for Measure,* tellingly, appears to be the earliest example of the word in the ironic sense.

24. I have moved the entry direction. Lever does not accept the Folio's "Scena Tertia" but mistakenly follows its accordant placement of the entry. But "What's to do here?" shows where it ought to be in the staging. Where F places it shows that its "Scena Tertia" is imposed by someone other than the playwright.

25. Tillyard's error about the relation of earlier and later parts of the scene

appears with a fresh face in Gary Taylor and John Jowett, *Shakespeare Reshaped* (Oxford: Clarendon Press, 1993), chapter 3, 151ff., in which they attempt to bear out the contention of Dover Wilson in A. Quiller-Couch and J. Dover Wilson, ed., *Measure for Measure,* the New Cambridge Shakespeare (Cambridge: University of Cambridge Press, 1922) that the opening of I.ii—from TLN 96–171—is "an unShakespearian interpolation." They make much of the double account of Claudio's arrest, supposing only Pompey's to be Shakespearean. But this double report is nothing like that of Portia's death in *Julius Caesar.* N. W. Bawcutt, ed., *Measure for Measure,* the Oxford Shakespeare (Oxford: Clarendon Press, 1991), 73, sees that "the double account need not indicate revision" and emphasizes the importance of Mistress Overdone's detailed exposition, including the key fact that Claudio has been sentenced to death. Indeed, without that exposition we would not yet have heard of Claudio's existence and could not know that Pompey obliquely refers to him. Jowett and Taylor persistently refer to "the duplicate revelation of Claudio's crime and arrest." In fact the accounts are complementary, as also (as they do not note) are the references to the proclamation. We first hear of that from the 1 Gentleman who, without explanation, briefly suggests there might be a connection between it and Claudio's arrest. Pompey's figurative glance at Claudio's offence and arrest is at once followed by his informing the bawd of the proclamation as it affects the houses of resort. Again, Jowett and Taylor think Lucio appears oddly "ignorant of his friend's fate" since the bawd has "just given him the information he seeks." But Lucio's exit line as he rushes off is, "Away: lets goe learne the truth of it" (TLN 171). "His persistent and apparently perverse attentions" (we are told) "go beyond any need to verify Overdone's story"—but not beyond any need to focus and comment on Claudio's own views of his situation. They claim the scene's opening dialogue is typical of the comic stuff and bawdy used to pad out adaptations. Yet they later admit "that the conversation between Lucio and the Gentlemen is thematically relevant." However, they think "any discussion of sex and sin could claim as much" and, besides, "an interpolator may be credited with enough intelligence to contrive some relationship between what he adds and what is already here." But if the relationship involves a thematic relevance crucial to what is found later in the play—and that is the case—the contriver is more likely to be the author. They object that Shakespeare doesn't begin a second scene this way. He certainly never did one that began as this one must with the supposedly interpolated opening removed.

> *[Enter Clowne.]*
>
> Bawd. . . . How now? what's the newes with you.
>
> Clo. Yonder man is carried to prison.
>
> Baw. Well: what has he done?
>
> Clo. A Woman.
>
> Baw. But what's his offence.
>
> Clo. Groping for Trowts in a peculiar Riuer.
>
> Baw. What? is there a maid with child by him?
>
> Clo. No: but there's a woman with maid by him:
> you haue not heard of the proclamation, haue you?
>
> Baw. What proclamation, man?

(TLN 174–83)

On the Folio page with this scene, sig. F1ᵛ, "It is clear that the compositor found he had too much material for his page: a fact which rather suggests that he was including some six or seven lines which the caster-off had not taken into account" (Lever, ed., *Measure*, xx). Taylor and Jowett try to use this circumstance in support of their contention (152–53), but that is admissable only if the governing critical judgments about the first twenty-three lines in the scene stand up to examination. I can see no merit to their argument for non-Shakespearean interpolation in this scene.

Pompey's image for the crime in his riddling Fool's routine—"Groping for Trowts, in a peculiar Riuer"—however vivid and delightfully surprising readers find it, has been something of an interpretative puzzle. Lever, ed., *Measure*, 13, takes *peculiar* as "own" so that the reference is to the offender's own wife; but "a peculiar" is not *his* peculiar. N. W. Bawcutt, ed., *Measure for Measure*, the Oxford Shakespeare (Oxford: Clarendon Press, 1991), 96, sees that the image is of poaching (by the method of "tickling" trout), but is puzzled that the line would thus "appear to mean 'seducing other men's wives', which does not accurately describe Claudio's offence." The solution is that in fornication the river is privately owned though the woman is no one's wife. There is no specific commandment in "the table" against fornication. That prohibition is regularly understood in religious writings to be included in the commandment against adultery.

26. Tillyard, *Problem Plays*, 123–24. A yet-more-vehement earlier expression of this view is provided by Arthur Quiller-Couch (in A. Quiller-Couch and J. Dover Wilson, ed., *Measure for Measure*, xxxix): "We say confidently that the two parts could not have been written by the same man, at one spell, on one inspiration, or with anything like an identical or even continuous poetic purpose."

27. Tillyard, *Problem Plays*, 125.

28. Ibid. The edition for the Oxford Shakespeare by Bawcutt is the first to print III.i as a single scene with continuous line numbering.

29. Lever, ed., *Measure*, 14, quoting Henry Smith, *The Magistrates Scripture* (*Sermons*, 1591, 702): "The prince is like the great Image of God, the Magistrates are like little Images of God." See on the counterfeiting R. J. Kaufmann, "Bond Slaves and Counterfeits: Shakespeare's *Measure for Measure*," *Shakespeare Studies* 3 (1967): 85–97.

30. "Comic literal enactment" means that the symbolic has been given concrete form to make the literal action an incarnative enactment of its own significance. I develop an understanding of this dramatic method, in anticipation of its availability in the native tradition to the Elizabethans, in a study of the Wakefield Master's *Second Shepherds Play*: "Symbol and Structure in the *Secunda Pastorum*," *Comparative Drama* 1 (1967–68): 122–43; rpt. in *Medieval English Drama: Essays Critical and Contextual*, ed. Jerome Taylor and Alan H. Nelson (Chicago: University of Chicago Press, 1972), 177–211.

31. Rossiter, *Angel with Horns*, 163.

32. Ibid.

33. L. C. Knights, "The Ambiguity of *Measure for Measure*," *Scrutiny* 10 (1942): 222–33.

34. A. D. Nuttall, "Quid Pro Quo," *Shakespeare Studies* 4 (1951): 231–51.

35. Rossiter, *Angel with Horns*, 154–55. Another critic who sees the play to be "based on absurdity, like *The Mikado*" is Josephine Waters Bennett, "*Measure for Measure*" as *Royal Entertainment* (New York: Columbia University Press, 1966), 158.

36. A tapestry in the famous Redemption of Man series produced in Brussels, a copy of which Cardinal Wolsey ordered "for the legates chaumbre in Hampton courte" in 1521, is a fine instance. The strong group dominating the left of the tapestry's lower register shows personified Mercy preventing Justice from slaying

with her sword sinful Homo, who is surprised lying in the lap of Luxuria. In the register directly above, the Four Daughters of God consider his sin as depicted on a cloth where he is seen with a nude woman, presumably the one, clothed, with whom he is engaged in amorous conversation to the left. Homo's typical sin is "fornication." At top center of the tapestry, Justice and Mercy with His other Virtues debate his case before the throne of the triune deity. For a reproduction of this tapestry, see Heinrich Göbel, *Handteppiche* (Leipzig: Klinkhardt and Biermann, 1923), vol. 1 and D. T. B. Wood, "Tapestries of *The Seven Deadly Sins.*" *Burlington Magazine* 20 (1912): 210–22, 277–89. See frontispiece.

37. See John Hooper, *Later Writings,* ed. Charles Nevinson, the Parker Society (Cambridge, 1852), 138; John Dod and Robert Cleaver, *A plaine and familiar exposition of the ten commandments* (London, 1622), 187; Edwin Sandys, *Sermons,* ed. Joseph Ayre, the Parker Society (Cambridge, 1841), 325; Hugh Latimer, *Works,* ed. George Elwes Corrie, 2 vols., the Parker Society (Cambridge, 1844), 1: 170; 244; Thomas Becon, *The Catechism,* ed. Joseph Ayre, the Parker Society (Cambridge, 1844), 371. Cf. Henry Bullinger, *The christen state of matrimony* (London, 1543), Diiii^r–[D6]^r; Henry Smith, *A preparatiue to marriage* (London, 1591), 45–47.

38. See Rosalind Miles, *The Problem of "Measure for Measure": A Historical Investigation* (London: Vision, 1976), 167–70. Gless, *Law and the Convent,* 64ff., is quite right to remark that critics have ignored the play's insistent emphasis *by costume* on the regular clergy.

39. Gless sees that "the poet makes it very plain that this portion of his play belongs to the genre of antimonastic satire" and, in the light of Christian "liberty" (Gal. 5: 1 and 4: 3), the convent represents imprisonment and "bondage" as much as Claudio's "captivity" (*Law and the Convent,* 98–99). The Duke's words to Angelo in I.i about Nature's requiring thanks and use apply to Isabella, too.

40. Ibid., 105–6: Gless emphasizes "The Christological (and Mariological) suggestions in Lucio's request" that she be an intercessor and that in this passage "Shakespeare manipulates his diction to evoke larger meanings."

41. Ibid., 132.

42. As will be apparent, I intend no more appeal to a Bakhtinian conception than, from a different viewpoint, does Charles Swann, "Lucio: benefactor or malefactor," *Critical Quarterly* 29 (1987): 55–70. As he says, "there is little suggestion here of *positive* 'ludic carnivalesque'" (56). But we differ as to the reasons for this. Jonathan Dollimore, "Transgression and surveillance in *Measure for Measure,*" in Dollimore and Alan Sinfield, eds., *Political Shakespeare: New Essays in Cultural Materialism* (Manchester: Manchester University Press, 1985), 72–87, also rejects such a Bakhtinian interpretation, but "as scarcely less inappropriate than that which privileged 'true' authority over anarchic desire" (73). He reads the ending as "a reactionary fantasy": "not a cancelling of authoritarianism so much as a fantasy resolution of the very fears from which authoritarianism partly grows . . . ; the very disclosure of social realities which make progress seem imperative is recuperated in comedic closure, a redemptive wish-fulfillment of the status-quo." Thus, the play's "transgressors . . . signify neither the unregeneracy of the flesh, nor the ludic carnivalesque. Rather, as the spectre of unregulated desire, they are exploited to legitimate an exercise in authoritarian repression" (83–84). Swann, refreshingly, finds this "to be, quite simply, wrong in its suggestion that the end offers a unified ideological message" (56).

43. Some think Elbow's "his face" (83) can be construed to refer to Froth, the proposed customer; and sometimes it has been so played. But the context

concerns Mrs. Overdone's "means"—as Elbow understands that, her pimp, Pompey.

44. See, e.g., Arthur Dent, *A sermon of repentaunce* (London, 1582) sig. Bj^v: "But where is thy Repentaunce thou miserable wretche? Doest thou thinke that Gods mercie is common to all? And Christe death a Baude to thy sinnes?" *STC* lists no less than thirty-seven further editions of this popular book by 1638. It is most odd that Gless, *Law and the Convent*, 139, has nothing to say of this background. Bawcutt, ed., in the 1991 Oxford, for the first time cites *OED bawd* sb., sense b ["He who or that which panders to any evil design or vicious practice"], the parallel *OED* quotes from 1607 ["The mercy of God . . . is made a bawd to all manner of ungodliness"], and refers us to the passage in *Richard II*. But the centrality of the idea in the play is unremarked. The Tourneur text cited is *The Revenger's Tragedy,* ed. Lawrence J. Ross, Regents Renaissance Drama (Lincoln: University of Nebraska Press, 1966).

45. See *Othello,* ed. Lawrence J. Ross (Indianapolis: Bobbs Merrill, 1974), 192, quoting in connection with IV.i.161–62 the official homily on adultery: "Bee yee holy, for I am holy. Hitherto haue we heard how greeuous a sinne fornication and whoredome is and howe greatly God doeth abhorre it. . . ." In *Certaine sermons, or homilies, appoynted by the Queenes Maiestie* (London, 1595) 1: sig. [K7]^v.

46. Citing *The Geneva Bible*: A Facsimile of the 1560 Edition with an Introduction by Lloyd E. Berry. (Madison: University of Wisconsin Press, 1969).

47. *The City of God,* trans. Marcus Dods (New York: Modern Library, 1950), XIV.17 (465).

In all the fallen Adam's descendants, "the organs of generation are so subjected to the rule of lust, that they have no motion but what it communicates." No longer are these members "moved by authority of the will"; they can be controlled only after the rebelliously involuntary appetitive motion (Augustine). Hence this involuntary "natural" motion in man's flesh was seen as the typical consequence of his will's being turned from God, and therefore as a prime symbol of his unregenerate nature, a mark of original sin and of mankind's need of grace. The Ninth of the Thirty-Nine Articles, of original sin, states, "And this infection doth remayne, yea in them that are regenerated, whereby the luste of the flesh . . . is not subject to the lawe of God." (*Articles* [1571], in *Synodalia,* ed. Edward Cardwell, 2 vols. [Oxford, 1842] 1: 93–94.) The wording of this article results from the same circumstance that provided Augustine with an authoritative basis for his interpretation: the fact that already in Scripture "Concupiscence [is] taken for all our corrupt affections" (from The Table in the Genevan *New Testament* [London, 1577] fol. 435^v).

48. Paul Hammond, "The Argument of *Measure for Measure,*" *English Literary Renaissance* 16 (1986): 500.

49. This meaning is commonplace in *allegoriae* for the "detestable oak" of which Bersuire writes: "Et ista pro certo est vir peccator, qui proprie dicitur quercus quia durusa est. . . ." See, s.v. *quercus* in Petrus Berchorius, *Opera omnia,* 6 vols. (Coloniae Agrippinae, 1731), *Dictionarium moralis* 5: 367, wrongly numbered 377. This symbolism appears in art, too. The oak leaf cluster so prominently sported by the specimen of humanity with a face full of *Schadenfreude* at Christ's left in Bosch's *The Crowning with Thorns* (National Gallery, London) is a striking instance.

50. *Measure for Measure, A New Variorum Edition,* ed. Mark Eccles (Modern Language Association of America, 1980), 93. Henceforth cited as *New Variorum.*

51. William Empson, "Sense in *Measure for Measure*," *The Structure of Complex Words* (London: Chatto and Windus, 1951), 274, cited *New Variorum*, 93.

52. Gless, *Law and the Convent*, 112–13.

53. Miles, *Problem of "Measure,"* 177.

54. *New Variorum*, 100.

55. I agree with those, like Alexander Leggatt, "Substitution in *Measure for Measure*," *Shakespeare Quarterly* 39 (1988): 344, who think Shakespeare actually wrote "God in my mouth" in line 4. There are forty-four *heauen/heauens/heauen*'s in the text but not a single instance of *God*, which has a particular propriety here. That the play appears to have been expurgated could support Taylor and Jowett's argument that a later promptbook than the original served as the copy for Crane's transcript. But it does not follow that that promptbook had been interpolated. Bawcutt, ed., *Measure*, considers the possibility that Crane himself was the censor if there indeed was censorship in *Measure*, in which case he thinks "he must have been working from uncensored foul papers" (69).

56. This manner of understanding the import of what is the most specific reference to King James—*n.b.* "king" (27)—is (I believe) new to the critical discussion about reference to the monarch in the play. Lever, ed., *Measure*, xxxiii–xxxiv, in discussing the reference in this passage to the incident during James's would-be secret visit to the Exchange in March 1604, reasonably denies Dover Wilson's assumption that 26–30 "form a kind of postscript to Angelo's speech; for these lines produce a further likeness developing that which precedes, 24–26." The speech coheres:

> O heavens,
> Why does my blood thus muster tò my heart,
> Making both it unable for itself
> And dispossessing all my other parts
> Of necessary fitness?
> So play the foolish throngs with one that swounds,
> Come all to help him, and so stop the air
> By which he should revive; and even so
> The general subject to a well-wish'd king
> Quit their own part, and in obsequious fondness
> Crowd to his presence, where their untaught love
> Must needs appear offence.

                                                                    (19–30)

What remains unnoticed is that these two figures move the mind away from what Angelo is *experiencing* in his disturbed little state of man, and increasingly draw attention to the thought developed *about* what he is experiencing. (Indeed, it might well be played as evasion, as the trained mind trying to deal with the ordering principle of something because the disorder being experienced is too distressing.) That move is deliberately climaxed with clear reference to something Shakespeare's original audience (and certainly the one including the King at the first recorded performance) would have known had happened to the sovereign in London but months before. Robert Armin, of Shakespeare's company, claimed to have written *The Time Triumphant* (1604), a tract about the King's progress through London, which includes a description of the incident at the Exchange (supposedly from the observation of Armin's kinsman Gilbert Dugdale, under whose name the tract was published). This even purports to tell us what the King vehemently said at the time, *inter alia,*

. . . you will say perchance it is your loue, will you in loue presse vpon your Souereigne thereby to offend him, your Souereigne perchance mistake your loue and punish it as an offence, but heare me when hereafter [he] comes by you, doe as they doe in Scotland stand still, see all, and vse silence. . . .

(B2)

Shakespeare knew such report. What that means for his play, whose duke goes unrecognized, "a looker-on here in Vienna" until accidentally disclosed and identified, is that we must with the greatest circumspection consider *the silence* of his subjects when this prince pronounces his resolution of the action. *The Time Triumphant* and its significance for the play were noted independently by J. W. Lever, "The Date of *Measure for Measure*," *Shakespeare Quarterly* 10 (1959): 381–84 and David L. Stevenson, "The Role of James I in Shakespeare's *Measure for Measure*," *ELH* 26 (1959): 191–93. The latter subject is further considered below, in n. 85.

57. Gless, *Law and the Convent*, 126–29. Gless sees "that Angelo's temptation is especially diabolic because it requires complicity. Isabella must *choose* sin" (127).

58. Ibid., 132–35. Sharply observing her spiritual carnality, Gless points out that "she, like her brother, can be considered faithless" (133). There is irony at the expense of the speaker when she hurls "O faithless coward!" at her "brother" (III.i.136).

59. Arthur Kirsch, *Shakespeare and the Experience of Love* (Cambridge: Cambridge University Press, 1981), 91.

60. Leavis, "Greatness of *Measure*," 243.

61. Hammond, *The Argument*, 504–5.

62. William Hazlitt, *Characters of Shakespeare's Plays* (London: Oxford University Press, 1959), 245.

63. See Lever, ed., *Measure*, lxxxvii–lxxxviii. Hammond points out that Claudio's passionate "subchristian speech would have been scorned by classical philosophers. It was precisely such disreputable arguments about the fate of body or spirit after death that Lucretius exposed" ("The Argument," 506).

64. Tillyard, *Problem Plays*, 128.

65. I follow Pope in punctuating with a comma here. Lever stands on the Folio in printing a semicolon, on the ground that its "omission . . . makes 'remedy' unnecessarily ambiguous." But it *is* ambiguous.

66. See William Witherle Lawrence, *Shakespeare's Problem Comedies* (New York: Macmillan, 1931). Marliss C. Desens, *The Bed-Trick in English Renaissance Drama: Explorations in Gender, Sexuality, and Power* (Newark: University of Delaware Press; London and Toronto: Associated University Presses, 1994), 37–38, observes that bed-tricks were not being used on the English stage prior to the late 1590s, and thus finds problematical the widely current "assumption that dramatists and their audiences would have considered it a convention of comedy." She notes that questionable assumption "exists side by side with the realization that *All's Well that Ends Well* and *Measure for Measure* are departures from the romantic comedies of the 1580s and 1590s." In nondramatic literature before the motif's appearance on the stage, she finds that "writers apparently do not associate the bed-trick exclusively with any one genre."

67. Herbert S. Weil Jr., "The Options of the Audience: Theory and Practice in Peter Brook's *Measure for Measure*," *Shakespeare Survey* 25 (1972): 31: "It is difficult to believe that any actor could emerge from the dialogue with Lucio and

still retain the charisma of an ideal ruler." That is not only right, but as Swann says, "particularly right to emphasize performance" ("Lucio," 63).

68. Cf. *King Lear* IV.iv.22–23 and S. L. Bethell, *Shakespeare and the Popular Dramatic Tradition* (Durham, N.C.: Duke University Press, 1944), 60. Incidentally, I reject as an unwarranted embroidery the staging of the entrance of Escalus, Provost, and Bawd at III.ii.183, adopted by Lever, originally proposed by Lascelles, *Shakespeare's "Measure,"* 93 and n. 3.

69. For a defense of the Duke's soliloquy concluding III.i., see N. W. Bawcutt, "'He Who the Sword of Heaven will Bear': the Duke versus Angelo in *Measure for Measure,"* *Shakespeare Survey* 37 (1984): 89–98.

70. Taylor and Jowett, *Shakespeare Reshaped,* 119ff., elaborately develop Alice Walker's proposal, that the first twenty-three lines of IV.i were interpolated by another hand for a revival, made in her last publication, "The Text of *Measure for Measure,"* *The Review of English Studies* 34 (1983): 5. The argument first assumes the authority behind the Folio text of the play is a promptbook. But copy for F probably was a Ralph Crane transcript which has masked the nature of *his* copy. Bawcutt, ed., *Measure,* 74–75, thinks "There are some signs of revision, but not sufficiently thoroughgoing to render the play ready for production." He therefore treats F "as basically a foul-papers text." Greg favors this view (W. W. Greg, *The Shakespeare First Folio* [Oxford: Clarendon Press, 1955], 356); but Evans, ed., *Riverside,* 585, allows that "There are, at any rate, no confusions in the F1 text serious enough to rule out a prompt-copy source." The matter is most uncertain; Taylor and Jowett's case for prompt-copy has its strengths but is not I think decisive. And they have then to prove, in the absence of evidence for a post-Shakespearean revival, that Crane's copy was a revised promptbook, and one in which interpolations had been made. Hence their desire to place the staging of the text at Blackfriar's, where such a revival would have occurred. IV.i probably opens with a discovery and their claim is that "none of the conventions of the outdoor theatres would call for a discovery here" and that this one better fits the conventions of the Blackfriars (not used by the King's Men until 1609–10) "than it fits those associated with the Globe, in 1603–4" (135). There is nothing to this. The song is not music between acts, and Shakespeare calls in *Othello,* the same year as *Measure,* for I.iii to open with a discovery of seated figures (with no more than a table) and for III.i to begin with instrumental music.

A version of the song with a second stanza is found in *Rollo* (now probably dated 1617) in a scene usually ascribed to Fletcher. This has raised inevitable questions about priority. Was the first stanza of the *Rollo* song interpolated in *Measure* or derived from it? These scholars reject discriminations of poetic differences in the two stanzas as merely subjective value judgments. But I do not consider so dismissable critical strictures such as those by John D. Jump, ed., *Rollo Duke of Normandy, or The Bloody Brother* (Liverpool: University Press of Liverpool, 1948). But let the reader judge.

> Take o take those lipps away,
> That so sweetly were forsworne,
> And those eyes like break of day,
> Lights that doe mislead the morne,
> But my kisses bring againe,
> Seales of love though seal'd in vaine.
>
> Hide o hide those hills of Snow,
> That thy frozen bosome beares,
> On whose tops the pinks that grow

Are yet of those that April wears,
But first set my poore heart free,
Bound in those Icy chaines by thee.

Consider the transformation of the frozen bosom with hills of snow into those icy chains that bind the lover. The chains, or *catenae amoris,* are conventional enough, but the pronoun is lax and the figure strained in a manner quite at odds with anything in the first stanza. Like Lever, I think it probable that Fletcher returned to the popular model (where *luxus nivei pectoris* was to be found) to extend Shakespeare's lyric.

What *is* merely subjective, and convenient, is the assertion that "the song in *Measure* cannot be called necessary to its context" (132). Taylor and Jowett reject Walker's judgment that the song is "an artistic blunder," but they find suspect that "the play contains no other songs, no other passages of romantic poetry, and (rather surprisingly) not a single kiss." (Who should kiss? Here we may feel our collective leg is being pulled.) "Mariana's melancholy serves no further function in the plot, and does not characterize her speeches or conduct hereafter"; but her case is being altered in this scene! "Mariana's plight, and the sympathy she deserved, have already been made abundantly clear to us by the Duke; the modesty and good will of her speeches when she enters later in IV.i would make an equally favorable first impression on an audience." The writers are confusing dramatic preparation and required introduction of a character not seen before. Romance and Mariana's stasis in melancholy rejection need to be economically represented before the Duke's proposal of the bed-trick. That her role after her reentry suffices to represent what they conceive to be the main points to be made about her won't wash at all. After the opening grouping and the succeeding one with the Friar, Mariana has one line after Isabella's entry, is then offstage for twenty-five lines, has three brief lines with Isabella and the Friar, is off again while the Duke briefly soliloquizes; and when they rejoin him she has exactly three words in the twelve lines concluding the scene. The expression of her situation and most of her speech is in the song and the dialogue with the Friar that grows out of it. Her muted part after her reentry, without what is accomplished in the opening twenty-three lines, simply will not serve.

The very first function of her speech there is to establish her trust in the Friar's counsel. She at once identifies him as "a man of comfort," which (since we know what the Duke-Friar is about) reawakens the examination of conflicting senses of "comfort" in the opening groupings of III.i; and then she specifies: "whose aduice / Hath often still'd my brawling discontent." Walker (4) found a difficulty here since the Duke assumed his Friar role "so recently." Taylor and Jowett, while admitting the contradiction might "be Shakespeare's fault," think "such an anomaly in a passage otherwise suspect does little to encourage confidence in the text's authenticity" (137). Why "fault"? The discrepancy shows up in the study, not in the theater. This is no more a "fault" than the "double time" in *Othello,* a much more obvious contradiction though it took readers until the middle of the nineteenth century to notice it. What these disintegrators symptomatically do not observe is that there is an important line late in the scene that presupposes the point of what Mariana has said of the Friar in her second and third lines: "She'll take the enterprise upon her, father, / If you advise it" (66–67). That puts the onus of the matter on the "Friar," where it belongs.

The romance elements early in the scene these scholars too narrowly conceive, one consequence being that they misconstrue the stylistic difference from the next part of the scene (137–38). Those elements are needed for the ironies engendered by the proposal of the bed-trick—which is never mentioned by Taylor and Jowett though that is the scene's business and focus. They can suppose the song (with what follows) unnecessary because they entertain no conception of its functions. The scene patently is incomplete without those first two groupings. That is why IV.i *cannot remain a scene* in their reconstruction of what existed before the conjectured interpolation.

The two-stanza lyric in *Rollo* was very popular, as evidenced by its appearance in numerous manuscript and printed songbooks. Its setting by Robert Wilson, very likely composed for that play, does not accommodate the echoic repetitions in the *Measure* lyric ("Bring againe" and "seal'd in vaine"). Nor would that sort of repetition be possible with the second stanza in *Rollo*. No problem. "The extant music could easily be altered to accommodate a repetition" of the phrases in *Measure* "or might easily have been altered to replace those repetitions with a repetition of the last two lines instead" (131). "Could be" and "might have been" establish nothing. If someone wished to interpolate the first stanza from *Rollo* into a revival production of *Measure,* why alter the lyric so that the available music would have to be changed? Yet these writers see that "the Folio's repetitions . . . , as much as anything, create the impression that the song fits Mariana's situation" (130). What an insightful interpolator! And he also by these means (and context) altered this derivative from *Ad Lydiam* so that the forsaken one is implied to be a woman. Interestingly, Shakespeare made the same alteration of the received "old thing" that he turned into the Willow Song sung by Desdemona in *Othello* IV.iii.

Indeed, the song conjectured to have been interpolated in IV.i fits the context in *Measure* better than the two-stanza lyric fits the context in *Rollo*. Taylor and Jowett put as good a face on the song as they can, as "the final ingredient in this sensual stew" prepared by Edith in her plot to take revenge on Rollo, the murderer of her father, by using his passion for her to catch him off guard. But only the second stanza rather frigidly exposes breasts and nipples while the male suitor is bound in the icy chains of rejection by her frozen bosom. "As a dramatic device the song allows Edith to tempt Rollo without explicitly offering herself to him" (132–33). Their claim is that "the song deliberately titivates"; but one would suppose the suitor-in-the-song's complaint of the beloved's betrayal and vow-breaking scarcely suited to "inflaming Rollo's lust." Of course it could be construed to hint Edith's treachery.

The dialogue about the music immediately following the song in *Measure,* Taylor and Jowett also consider interpolated. They say, truly enough, that in Shakespeare "the effects of music are almost always beneficial" (139). But they are ignoring the broken music and Pandar's song on love in *Troilus* and the suspect wind-music aubade in *Othello* III.i. See Frederick W. Sternfeld, *Music in Shakespearean Tragedy,* rev. ed. (London and New York: Kegan Paul and Dover Press, 1967) and Lawrence J. Ross, "Shakespeare's 'Dull Clown' and Symbolic Music," *Shakespeare Quarterly* 17 (1966): 107–28. "Charm" (in the Duke's observation, "music oft hath such a charm / To make bad good, and good provoke to harm" [14–15]), is a powerful word in Shakespeare's English, the reference being to music's oft-noted power to draw the spirits. The poet who showed in *The Merchant of Venice* so compendious a knowledge of ideas about music and its ethos was hardly unaware of the anciently criticized effects of certain modalities, instruments, and uses of music. These scholars think it odd that the Duke's speech is a couplet; but here is a *sententia* about a type of music that can (as Lever says) "give sin a pleasing aspect and lead virtue into harm," or to put it more technically, a *sententia* about use of a power to draw that can give evils the admixture or appearance of good needed to make them objects capable of provoking the errant will to harmful choice. Such a *sententia* is not impertinent to a play deeply concerned with the traditional theme of the use and abuse of things, with the power even of virtue to tempt to sin, with our corrupt nature's pursuit of a thirsty evil in fulfilling our sexuality. Of course music and love are manifestly and traditionally paired and analogized. Taylor and Jowett object that music "is not provoking goodness to any discernible harm in this scene, or this play." But that is entirely to miss the point by failing to see the relevance of the Duke's sentence to what we know is his plan for Mariana and its moral ambiguity. It is crucially telling that Taylor and Jowett's discussion never even looks at the concluding and climactic speech of the scene any more than it concerns itself with the bed-trick.

71. Lascelles, *Shakespeare's "Measure,"* 107, and Lever, ed., *Measure,* xx–xxi, 99. The idea that a covering speech for an offstage conference must be "long enough" betrays an errant expectation of literal plausibility from Shakespearean representation that absurdly confines his, and our, imaginative freedom. The last we hear before the battle in *King Lear* V.ii, after Edgar has told his father, "Pray that the right may thrive," is Gloucester's "Grace go with you, sir!" at Edgar's exit. What follows is a breathtaking simplification.

> *Alarum and retreat within. Enter* [Edgar].
>
> *Edg.*   Away, old man, give me thy hand, away!
> King Lear hath lost, he and his daughter ta'en.
>
> (2–6)

Productions usually try to lengthen "the battle" with sound effects offstage or even choreographed combat onstage. But that is to misunderstand. The battle as event is indicated; the dramatic representation is focused on the contrast between the hope and prayer preceding and the outcome disappointing both. How long should Claudio and Isabella have for his mimed asking of his sister's pardon and their reconciliation? Five lines is what they get (III.i.172–77). Instances differ. It has got to be significant that I have yet to encounter any objector to the brevity of the Duke's covering speech for Isabella and Mariana's conversation within who also observes that the brevity *of their conference* has been dramatically prepared: "I shall attend your leisure; but make haste, / The vaporous night approaches" (IV.i.57–58). The same need for briskly getting on with the bed-trick plan is repeated (with fresh irony) at the scene's close, "Come, let us go; / Our corn's to reap, for yet our tithe's to sow" (75–76). We must remember this when Taylor and Jowett, supposedly reconstructing what Shakespeare originally wrote, substitute for the Duke-Friar's present covering speech a twenty-four-line speech by him found elsewhere in the play.

Taylor and Jowett are sure the Duke's short soliloquy in IV.i is "inappropriate," but they realize that it is a "discrete unit" and could not have been, as Warburton and followers suppose, originally part of a single speech with his earlier soliloquy on calumny at III.i.444–47. They agree the lines are undoubtedly by Shakespeare, but are confident he did not intend them as the covering speech during Isabella and Mariana's withdrawal in IV.i. "The speech is irrelevant to that context and unusually short to cover the unheard dialogue of the two women" (121). This untested assertion, which will soon first be used to support interpolation of the song from *Rollo,* is itself supported only by an astonishing drum-fire iteration claiming a consensus for it: "almost all critics feel"; "No one is satisfied with the speech"; "almost everyone regards it as a striking maladministration of Shakespeare's text"; "as has been almost universally accepted," etc. (121–22). There was a time, and a very long time it was, when it was almost universally accepted that the sun went around the earth.

A covering speech during the women's withdrawal in IV.i is still needed. What to do? They elaborate a proposal, for which there is no consensus, briefly developed by Kenneth Muir, "The Duke's Soliloquies in *Measure for Measure*," *Notes and Queries* 211 (1966): 135–36, that the Duke's long soliloquy now concluding III.i was the original covering speech. They argue that "He who the sword of heaven would bear" ends nothing and properly belongs where the "O place and greatness" speech appears in F. The latter short soliloquy they conjecture belongs after the Duke's conversation with Escalus and just preceding Isabella's entry presently at IV.i.20. In other words, they suppose that before later interpolation there was no distinct scene, IV.i. In Shakespeare's original they imagine III.i continued straight through to conclude with the Duke's speech ending IV.i in F (140ff.). That would make III.i a scene even longer than the play's extensive concluding one. But the attempt to justify the new context for "O place" and to find reference in it to Angelo as well as the Duke is singularly unconvincing. The interpolation of twenty-four lines of tetrameters ending with the absolute prediction "With Angelo tonight shall lie / His old betrothed" (III.i.271–72) while, having told the women to hasten, he awaits them to find out whether Mariana agrees to the plan, is dramatically absurd. For Taylor and Jowett the conjectured interpolator's putting "the sword of heaven" soliloquy at the close of III.i makes a "trumped up ending" that "breaks the back of an originally uninterrupted transition from tragicomedy to comedy" (140–41). But that is to argue that the proper conclusion of the six hundred-line movement supposedly accomplishing that is the Duke's speech explaining that bringing Mariana and Angelo together by the bed-trick is no sin.

It takes but one shot of irreducible evidence to bring down this speculative balloon. They see there is no cleared stage or new scene at Isabella's exit at III.i.270, and therefore no "III.ii," but suppose an implicit shift of locale from inside to outside the prison. With omission of the supposedly interpolated matter and the brief interval supplied by the six-line soliloquy from IV.i, Isabella then enters to the Duke.

> Isabella talks to the Duke, and he calls Mariana. Not until Mariana's entrance do we have any clear idea of the location of this dialogue: Shakespeare has carefully but unobtrusively shifted the locale out of the prison into the unlocalized outdoors, and by means of a series of encounters has created the impression that the Duke has moved. He probably knocks on the door when (at TLN 1823: 4.1.19) he calls 'what hoa, within; come forth'—a form of address appropriate enough if he has just arrived outside a house, and might expect a servant to answer. . . . (142)

That is not the way Shakespeare makes a major shift in locale and it is explicitly contradicted by the way he in fact has prepared for the change of locale that occurs. The evidence appears earlier in III.i, in a part of the play where Taylor and Jowett find no interpolation in the dramatist's work.

> *Duke.* . . . I will presently to Saint Luke's; there at the moated grange resides this dejected Mariana; at that place call upon me; and dispatch with Angelo, that it may be quickly.
>
> (III.i.264–8)

Taylor and Jowett have suppressed any reference to "the moated grange." But when, at the start of IV.i, we hear that song sung for a female character not seen in the play before, we know this must be "this dejected Mariana" and the place therefore the moated grange. When Isabella arrives there to meet with the Duke, the place must be as appointed, the moated grange. There is no way to get from the prison, inside or out, to the moated grange without a new scene. These writers on the play have not proved IV.i.1–23 interpolated; they have rewritten Shakespeare's play. What we are left to do is inquire into the validity of the methods by which they then proceed to attribute to Middleton interpolations in *Measure for Measure* that did not occur.

72. See the citations by Lever, ed., *Measure*, liv, from Henry Swinburne, *A Treatise of Spousals* (1686) and particularly for the presupposition of mutual consent, from William Perkins, *Of Christian Oeconomie*, chap. 4 (1617 ed.).

73. Ernest Schanzer, "The Marriage-Contracts in *Measure for Measure*," *Shakespeare Survey* 13 (1960): 89, n. 21.

74. Lever thinks that at 41–45 "F inexplicably distributes Abhorson's answer"—his proof that his profession is a mystery—"between the two speakers." But the clown's (Pompey's) explication of the gruff Abhorson's brief response to his demand for proof ("Every true man's apparel fits your thief") neatly marks the agreement of executioner and bawd explored since the Provost's comment at exit ". . . you weigh equally: a feather will turn the scale" (28–29). F's assignment of the speeches is ably defended by Gary Taylor, "*Measure for Measure*, IV.ii.41–46," *Shakespeare Quarterly* 29 (1978): 419–21.

75. "For we are said to sleepe, whilest wee continue in the state of vnregeneration. . . . And wee are then said to awake when we rise out of this estate, either in our first conuersion, or when we reuiue our repentance." John Downame, *A gvide to godlynesse, or a treatise of a Christian life* (London, 1622), 506–7; cf. Hugh Latimer, *Remains*, ed. George Elwes Corrie, the Parker Society (Cambridge, 1844), 13. The relation of repentance to apprehension of life as well as death "but as a drunken sleep" (141) is established at the introduction of Barnadine in the play (126–51). This Christian imagery takes off from Jesus' disappointment in the disciples he asked to watch with him at Gethesemane: "he came . . . & found them àsleepe" (Matt. 26:40–41). It is powerfully developed by St. Paul: " . . . *it is* nowe time that we should arise from sleepe, for nowe is our saluation neerer, then when we beleeued it. / The night is past, and the day is at hand, let vs therefore cast away the workes of darkenesse. . ." (Rom. 13:11–12). The mention of drunkenness amongst the latter (13:13) is more fully treated (and understood metaphorically as well as literally) in 1 Thess. 5:5–8. The following from Downame, *The Christian Warfare* (London, 1604) is typical:

> Now . . . the watchfulnes of the soule is when as wee doe not sleepe in our sinnes, being rocked in the cradle of securitie, but shake off our drowsines by vnfained repentance, rising vp to newnes of life. . . . Though therefore wee take our rest and sleepe in that measure which nature requireth, yet *let vs not sleepe as doe other* (to wit, in carnall securitie) *but let vs watch and be sober*, as it is Thess. 5.6. because in this respect it is time that we should arise from sleepe, for the darke night of ignorance is past; and the bright sunshine day of the Gospel is come, let vs therefore cast away the workes of darknes. (67)

That "it is almost clear dawn" (209) at the end of IV.ii is intensely ironic. This complex of Christian imagery, insistently emphasized in the literature of the period, is even to be found in ballad and printer's device. That editions, commentary, and interpretation—including Christian interpretation—of *Measure for Measure* have nothing to say about it indicates something very important about Shakespeare studies.

76. Hammond, "The Argument," 516, citing *Stuart Royal Proclamations: vol. 1: Royal Proclamations of King James I 1603–1625,* ed. James F. Larkin and Paul L. Hughes (Oxford: Clarendon Press, 1973), 23–27.

77. Lascelles, *Shakespeare's "Measure,"* 113, and Walter Raleigh, *Shakespeare,* English Men of Letters (New York: Macmillan, 1907), 148–49, cited *New Variorum,* 428. Lascelles is certain "that Barnadine was never intended to die in the play"; but she finds "no certainty, nor the hope of any," that "the qualities that have made him deathless . . . were part of Shakespeare's design"—a conclusion as sentimental as the one opposed.

78. Bawcutt, ed., *Measure,* in his 1991 Oxford continues this erroneous reassignment of the line.

79. Lever, ed., *Measure,* xxii–xxiii, thinks Lucio's anachronism (which very strangely is repeated at V.i.137–38) sorts with other anomalies, such as the Provost's failure to return though earlier told to do so swiftly (102–4), and that these point toward "a hasty and rather careless rewriting of the end of IV.iii, substituting Lucio's entry for the return of the Provost." To him "The awkward lingering of Isabella suggests that she was originally meant to depart before the intended arrival of the Provost." But that "awkward lingering" cannot be regarded an anomalous residue of an original intention; it is deliberate, as Lucio's address to her shows. Since the dramatic texts so often fail to note exits, the fact that F fails to specify an exit for Isabella cannot, I think, significantly figure in discussion of this matter.

80. See Lawrence Babb, "The Physiological Conception of Love in Elizabethan and Early Stuart Drama," *Publications of the Modern Language Association* 56 (1944): 1020–35.

81. Lever in the Arden does not, as Evans and Bawcutt do in their editions, add an entirely appropriate flourish to sort with this preparation at the start of the big entry for the grand final scene. This trumpeting suits the public return of the Duke and the formal heraldic stage picture he creates by taking Angelo and Escalus by the hand on either side, and it proclaims the theme of Fame which the Prince ironically develops about the eternal public report Angelo's "desert" merits (10–19).

82. For the import of Severus in the tradition behind the play, see Lever, ed., *Measure,* xliv–xlvi.

83. John Masefield, *William Shakespeare,* Home University Library (London, 1911), quoted *New Variorum,* 401.

84. G. Wilson Knight, *"Measure for Measure and the Gospels," in The Wheel of Fire* (1930), 4th rev. ed. (London: Methuen, 1949), 96.

85. That we have a substantial body of criticism that supposes the Duke to be the ideal prince and providence on earth is testimony to the subtlety with which Shakespeare has masked just how critical he has been of the feasibility of such a figure. The climax of this enterprise of the dramatist is his making the grand finale a play within the play, with the Duke as interior dramatist. We can already see in *Much Ado* what Shakespeare could critically accomplish with a duke in such a function. This enterprise also helps us with the thorny problem of the reference to King James I in *Measure for Measure.*
Lever would take a balanced view of the matter in saying "the case for some measure of identification [of Duke and King] is too strong to be discounted" (ed., *Measure,* xlviii). But that that measure is hard to pin down and so inviting of argument is consequent on what Shakespeare deliberately has done in the play. Because there is a guessing game *in the play* about the Duke, the game of application is that much more complicated and masked. There can be no doubt that

Shakespeare read the King's published writings in preparing to entertain his new
sovereign, and patron, and that *Basilicon Doron* echoes in the play. But Hammond
I think justly observes of the taking as flattery of the King the inclusion in *Measure for Measure* of many remarks which coincide with the monarch's views: "few
of the political assertions voiced in this play remain unchallenged by others or
uncompromised by events. The Duke's own role is carefully brought into question—although the Duke does not notice this, and perhaps James did not either"
("The Argument," 516). Indeed, I suspect much of the matter about slandering
the prince is smokescreen and the ending arranged to seem complimental of the
ruler's "aptness in remission" to cover the profound questioning in the play of
nothing less than such absolutist claims as were at the heart of the King's viewpoint. Swann argues, in work independent from Hammond's, that "the more skeptical or critical members of the audience (at once more critical of James and more
used to watching plays) could see a subtext in which the Duke's pretensions are
repeatedly exposed to examination" ("Lucio," 63). Swann writes with reference
to Lucio, the subject of his essay; but the examination begins in the first scene,
before Lucio is introduced. His great service is to make us look more closely at
two shrewdly critical contemporary views of two widely known instances early
in his reign in which King James made highly theatrical public demonstrations of
his Justice and Mercy as royal substitute of God on earth.

At Newark in April 1603 the King had sentenced a pickpocket to death but
then amnestied the prisoners in the Tower. Sir John Harington acidly commented:
"I hear our new King hath hanged one man before he was tryed; 'tis strangely
done: now if the wind bloweth thus, why may a man not be tryed before he hath
offended?" (Swann, "Lucio," 59). The clear significance to *Measure for Measure*
of the second instance, the *coup de théâtre* reprieve at the place of execution in
Winchester in the winter 1603–4 of those involved in the so-called Raleigh con-
spiracy, was first observed by Robert A. Shedd in an unpublished University of
Michigan dissertation (1953). Dudley Carleton reports the incident with remarkably sustained irony in a letter which, as Swann notes, has all too often been
cited in excerpts or without regard to its tone in studies of Shakespeare's play.
For the letter, dated Salisbury, 11 December 1603, see *Dudley Carleton to John
Chamberlain 1603–1624: Jacobean Letters,* ed. Maurice Lee Jr. (New Brunswick,
N.J.: Rutgers University Press, 1972), 47–52. After a number of executions, the
condemned conspirators, on the scaffold awaiting execution, were led off only to
be brought back later to confront the sheriff.

> Now all the actors being together on the stage (as use is at the end of a play) the sheriff
> made a short speech unto them, by way of the interrogatory of the heinousness of their
> offences, the justness of their trials, their lawful condemnation, and due execution there
> to be performed, to all which they assented; then, saith the sheriff, see the mercy of your
> prince, who of himself hath sent hither a countermand and given you your lives. . . .

Carleton emphasizes that "This resolution was taken by the king without man's
help, and no man can rob him of the praise of yesterday's action; for the lords
knew no other but that execution was to go forward till the very hour it should
be performed. . . ." James sustained till the last moment his tedious mystifying
about how, under various pressures to show mercy or to execute, *he* was going
to resolve the matter, even seeming "to lean to this side than the other by the
care he took to have the law take its course, and the execution hasted." Calling
his lords before him the King spoke, "travelling in contrarieties but holding the
conclusion in so indifferent balance that the lords knew not what to look for till

the end came out, 'and therefore I have saved them all.'" That plainly was the same King who told Parliament that "kings"

> are not only God's lieutenants upon earth and sit upon God's throne, but even by God Himself are called gods. . . . they make and unmake their subjects. They have power of raising and casting down, of life and of death, judges over all, and yet accountable to none but God only (D. H. Wilson, *King James VI and I* [London: Jonathan Cape, 1956], 179, cited Swann, "Lucio," 61).

This opinion underscores Carleton's diction as he tells of how the reaction starting with the addressed lords rippled through the court.

> The miracle was as great there as with us at Winchester and it took like effect: for the applause that began about the king went from thence into the presence and so round about the court.

At the performance at Winchester, Carleton drily reports,

> There was then no need to beg a plaudite of the audience, for it was given with such hues and cries that it went from the castle into the town and there began afresh. . . . And this experience was made of the difference of examples of justice and mercy, that in this last no man could cry loud enough, God save the king, and at the holding up of Brooke's head, when the executioner began the same cry, he was not seconded by the voice of any one man but the sheriff.

There is thus irony even about those who so applauded the Prince's conclusion of his play. Carleton, on the other hand, with the straightest of faces adds, as seeming afterthought before closing: "But one thing had like to have marred the play. . . ." The messenger bearing the King's pardon, John Gib ("a Scotch groom of the chamber"), had to be recalled because James (sitting no doubt on the throne of God) remembered he had not *signed* it. Yet another cross-adventure very nearly turned the royal play into a black and bloody farce, when Gib with the pardon "could not get so near the scaffold that he could speak to the sheriff but was thrust out amongst the boys and was fain to call out to Sir James Hay, or else Markham might have lost his neck."

However, I think Swann underrates Shakespeare's subtlety and misconceives his ends by leading us to suppose the critique of James to be the play's central burden. That can't be right unless we are ready to assume that Shakespeare was suicidal. There *was* that little matter a few years before of being called to account for giving that special performance of *Richard II* after "some of [Essex's] supporters had gone to the Globe and persuaded Augustine Phillips to revive" it on 7 February 1601—the day before the Essex Rebellion. Yet it appears, as Chambers says, that "little blame seems to have fallen upon the Chamberlain's men" (*William Shakespeare: A Study of the Facts and Problems,* 2 vols. [Oxford: Clarendon Press, 1930] 2: 354–55); but he notes the hint in *Hamlet* that the company may have "travelled for a time." Now in *Richard II* Shakespeare had developed the technique of powerfully expressing orthodox views to the satisfaction of any censor while variously calling them into profound question by context; but then he explodes the views in action of Bolingbroke, too. The dramatic structure is dialectical. *Measure for Measure* as much as *Hamlet* and *King Lear* has its roots in *Richard II.* In it Shakespeare's mind can (I think) be said to be working outward from the particular incarnations in his own time of what he is getting at more essentially.

86. Robert Ornstein, *The Moral Vision of Jacobean Tragedy* (Madison: University of Wisconsin Press, 1960), 258, cited *New Variorum*, 410.

87. See Henry Bullinger, *Decades*, trans. H. I., ed. Thomas Harding, 4 vols, the Parker Society (Cambridge, 1855), 4: 238; Thomas Becon, *Early Works*, ed. Joseph Ayre, the Parker Society (Cambridge, 1843), 12; John Dod and Robert Cleaver, *Exposition*, sig. [Aa7]ᵛ; Sandys, *Sermons*, 303–4.

88. Samuel Johnson (ed. 1765), in *New Variorum*, 268.

89. See *New Variorum*, 272.

90. That the Duke comes close to parodying surrender of her chastity to save a brother others have noted, e.g., Jocelyn Powell, "Theatrical *Tromp l'oeil* in *Measure for Measure*," *Shakespearian Comedy, Stratford-upon-Avon Studies* 14 (1972): 181–209.

91. As Lever, ed., *Measure*, observes, most editors give Lucio an exit *after line 521*, and he objects that this "distracts attention from the Duke's speech." Agreeing, Swann, "Lucio," 67, remarks, "Though this would be a nice subversive touch, I find it hard to believe it a good idea." But these students of the play are confusing two questions: Have editors rightly placed Lucio's exit? (to which the answer is no) and does Shakespeare's text call for Lucio to exit before the Duke concludes the play? (to which the answer is yes). Thus, Swann buys Lever's concluding processional exit with Lucio under guard bringing up the rear. Noting that the procession is by couples, he admits "Kate Keepdown isn't there (even if a Miller or a Brook could easily produce her—and what of a production that did just that?)." It would contradict the necessity that has the Duke command the Provost to "Proclaim . . . round about the city" for such an abused woman to come forward (506–10), that's what. The fact is that book-keepers had to be more concerned with getting entrances marked, not exits, and playwrights followed suit. The exit for Lucio would have been made explicit in rehearsal as it is clearly implicit in what Shakespeare set down to be performed. Having had the Duke say of Lucio, "Take him to prison" (518), what sense does it make for Shakespeare then to include Lucio in the inviting command, "So bring us to our palace" seventeen lines later (535)? Swann sees very clearly that the Duke's version of the ending as "a declaration and enactment of [his] power . . . is a fictive pseudoharmony" (68). What he does not see is how grave a mistake it is to tack the guarded Lucio at the end of that concluding procession to enforce the irony. We have been waiting for Lucio's comeuppance; he has already done his turn of upending the Duke's performance; and the mature Shakespeare does not drive such an effect into the ground. Nor need he do so. To resort to such overkill as Swann supposes is to deny Shakespeare, who has been ironic about the Duke since the play's first scene, the very opportunity he has created tactfully to expose the irony of the Duke's ending tacitly. That is an error arising from the need to oppose not only those who think the Duke and his ending splendid, but also those who object to both and imagine they have discovered something that Shakespeare did not deliberately do. It also arises from that itch, so typical of contemporary Shakespeare production, crudely to broaden effects to knock a mistrusted audience on the head with the point. It recurs in Swann when he asks, "What would happen if others joined Barnadine in refusing to play the game?" No such refusal is *enacted* here; nor is it the *Duke*'s game he has been given an opportunity to play. Swann sees the "challenge for the Friar in that coupling" of Barnadine and Friar Peter, but not the generalizing power of making that couple conclude the procession. The irony of that coupling is at the expense not merely of the Duke but of the audience as well.

92. Nuttall, "Quid Pro Quo," 239.

93. Hammond, "The Argument," 518.

94. Hawkins, *Likenesses*, 61, n. 8; "*Measure for Measure*," Twayne's New Critical Introductions to Shakespeare (Boston: Twayne, 1987), 32.

95. Swann, "Lucio," 67, says Juliet "certainly has something to say through her body" but he doesn't tell us what, and Shakespeare's text is not explicit on the point, for the emphasis in fact is elsewhere. If I were producing the play I would have her pregnant as before, not just to keep the audience from wondering where she has parked the newborn child offstage, but to support what *is* in the text: the exclusion of Claudio-Juliet from center stage as the romantic couple at the conclusion of the "comedy."

96. Gelb, "Illusion of Comedy," 31.

97. Miles, *Problems of "Measure,"* 136.

98. See *The Book of Common Prayer* (1559) in *Liturgies and Occasional Forms of Prayer set forth in the Reign of Queen Elizabeth,* ed. William Keatinge Clay, the Parker Society (Cambridge, 1847), 217, and see the basis in Eph. 5:22–23.

99. See *New Variorum,* 286. Swann sees in the last lines "the evasion of one kind of challenged power. It is patent mystification as the language of (challenged) power so often is" ("Lucio," 68).

100. Rossiter's essay, though I have noted important disagreements with it, is very fine and not least stimulating at its close. Though we must, I think, make some inevitable adjustment for the need of terms of understanding contingent upon the time and culture of the play's making, his is a compelling articulation of the play's greatness: "I can imagine *Measure for Measure* being read, for its humanity, its keen and subtle inquisition into man's nature (into justice and truth, sex and love), by humans in a remote future to whom all the Gospel references belong to a bygone myth—'a local faith called Christianity'—no nearer to them than the gods in Euripides. And I can imagine it holding them none the less, as *we* can be held by the human tangles of the Greek problem-playwright" (*Angel with Horns,* 170).

Works Cited

Augustine, Saint. *The City of God.* Translated by Marcus Dods. New York: The Modern Library, 1956.

Barton, Anne. Introduction to *Measure for Measure.* In *The Riverside Shakespeare.* Edited by G. Blakemore Evans. Boston: Houghton Mifflin, 1974.

Battenhouse, Roy W. "*Measure for Measure* and the Christian Doctrine of the Atonement." *Publications of the Modern Language Association* 61 (1946): 1029–59.

Bawcutt, N. W. "'He Who the Sword of Heaven will Bear': the Duke versus Angelo in *Measure for Measure.*" *Shakespeare Survey* 37 (1984): 89-98.

Becon, Thomas. *The Catechism.* Edited by Joseph Ayre. The Parker Society. Cambridge, 1844.

———. *Early Works.* Edited by Joseph Ayre. The Parker Society, Cambridge, 1843.

Bennett, Josephine Waters. "*Measure for Measure*" as *Royal Entertainment.* New York: Columbia University Press, 1966.

Berchorius, Petrus. *Opera omnia.* 6 vols. Coloniae Agrippinae, 1731.

Bethell, S. L. *Shakespeare and the Popular Dramatic Tradition.* Durham, N.C.: Duke University Press, 1944.

Bullinger, Henry. *The christen state of matrimony.* London, 1543.

———. *Decades.* Translated by H. I. Edited by Thomas Harding. 4 vols. The Parker Society. Cambridge, 1855.

Bullough, Geoffrey, ed. *Narrative and Dramatic Sources of Shakespeare.* Vol. 2: The Comedies 1597–1603. London: Routledge and Kegan Paul; New York: Columbia University Press, 1958.

Caputi, Anthony. "Scenic Design in *Measure for Measure*" (1962). In *Twentieth Century Interpretations of "Measure for Measure,*" edited by George L. Geckle. Englewood Cliffs, N.J.: Prentice Hall, 1970.

Carleton, Dudley. *Dudley Carleton to John Chamberlain 1603–1624: Jacobean Letters.* Edited by Maurice Lee Jr. New Brunswick, NJ: Rutgers University Press, 1972.

Certaine sermons, or homilies, appoynted by the Queenes Maiestie, to be declared and read, by all persones, vycars, and curates, euery Sunday and holy daye, in theyr churches, where thei haue cure. London, 1595.

Chambers, E. K. *William Shakespeare: A Study of the Facts and Problems.* 2 vols. Oxford: Clarendon Press, 1930.

Dent, Arthur. *A sermon of repentaunce.* London, 1595.

Desens, Marliss C. *The Bed-Trick in English Renaissance Drama: Explorations in Gender, Sexuality, and Power.* Newark: University of Delaware Press; London and Toronto: Associated University Presses, 1994.

Dod, John, and Robert Cleaver. *A plaine and familiar exposition of the ten commandments*. London, 1622.

Dollimore, Jonathan. "Transgression and surveillance in *Measure for Measure*." In Dollimore and Alan Sinfield, eds., *Political Shakespeare: New Essays in Cultural Materialism*. Manchester: Manchester University Press, 1985.

Downame, John. *The Christian Warfare*. London, 1604.

———. *A gvide to godlynesse, or a treatise of a Christian Life*. London, 1622.

Dugdale, Gilbert. *The Time Triumphant*. London, 1604. Reprinted in *Stuart Tracts 1603–1693*. Edited by C. H. Firth. In *An English Garner*. Vol. 2. London, 1903.

Edwards, Phillip. *Shakespeare and the Confines of Art*. London: Methuen, 1968.

Empson, William. "Sense in *Measure for Measure*." In *The Structure of Complex Words*. London: Chatto and Windus, 1951.

Evans, Bertrand. *Shakespeare's Comedies*. Oxford: Clarendon Press, 1960.

Frye, Northrop. *A Natural Perspective: The Development of Shakespearean Comedy and Romance*. New York: Columbia University Press, 1965.

Gelb, Hal. "Duke Vincentio and the Illusion of Comedy or All's Not Well that Ends Well." *Shakespeare Quarterly* 22 (1971): 25–34.

The Geneva Bible. A Facsimile of the 1560 Edition. With an Introduction by Lloyd E. Berry. Madison: University of Wisconsin Press, 1969.

Geneva *New Testament*. London, 1577.

Gless, Darryl J. *"Measure for Measure": The Law and the Convent*. Princeton: Princeton University Press, 1979.

Göbel, Heinrich. *Handteppiche*. 2 vols. Leipzig: Klickhardt and Biermann, 1923.

Greg, W. W. *The Shakespeare First Folio*. Oxford: Clarendon Press, 1955.

Haley, David. *Shakespeare's Courtly Mirror: Reflexivity and Prudence in "All's Well that Ends Well."* Newark: University of Delaware Press; London and Toronto: Associated University Presses, 1993.

Hammond, Paul. "The Argument of *Measure for Measure*." *English Literary Renaissance* 16 (1986): 496–519.

Hawkins, Harriet. *Likenesses of Truth in Elizabethan and Restoration Drama*. Oxford: Clarendon Press, 1972.

———. *"Measure for Measure."* Twayne's New Critical Introductions to Shakespeare. Boston: Twayne, 1987.

Hazlitt, William. *Characters of Shakespeare's Plays*. London: Oxford University Press, 1959.

Hooper, John. *Later Writings*. Edited by Charles Nevinson. The Parker Society. Cambridge, 1852.

Hunter, G. K., ed. *All's Well that Ends Well*. The Arden Shakespeare. London: Methuen, 1958.

John Phillip Kemble Promptbooks. Edited by Charles H. Shattuck. Folger Facsimiles: Promptbooks Series 1. 11 vols. Charlottesville: University Press of Virginia, 1974.

Jump, John D., ed. *Rollo Duke of Normandy, or The Bloody Brother*. Liverpool: University Press of Liverpool, 1948.

Kaufmann, R. J. "Bondslaves and Counterfeits: Shakespeare's *Measure for Measure*." *Shakespeare Studies* 3 (1967): 85–97.

Kirsch, Arthur. "The Integrity of *Measure for Measure.*" *Shakespeare Survey* 28 (1975) 89–105.

———. *Shakespeare and the Experience of Love.* Cambridge: Cambridge University Press, 1981.

Knight, G. Wilson. "*Measure for Measure* and the Gospels." In his *The Wheel of Fire.* 4th rev. ed. London: Methuen, 1949.

Knights, L. C. "The Ambiguity of *Measure for Measure.*" *Scrutiny* 10 (1942): 222–33.

Lascelles, Mary. *Shakespeare's "Measure for Measure."* London: Athlone Press, 1953.

Latimer, Hugh. *Works.* Edited by George Elwes Corrie. 2 vols. The Parker Society. Cambridge, 1844.

Lawrence, William Witherle. *Shakespeare's Problem Comedies.* New York: Macmillan, 1931.

Leavis, F. R. "The Greatness of *Measure for Measure.*" *Scrutiny* 10 (1942): 234–47.

Leggatt, Alexander. "Substitution in *Measure for Measure.*" *Shakespeare Quarterly* 39 (1988) 342–59.

Lever, J. W. "The Date of *Measure for Measure.*" *Shakespeare Quarterly* 10 (1959): 381–84.

———, ed. *Measure for Measure.* The Arden Shakespeare. London: Methuen, 1967.

Liturgies and Occasional Forms of Prayer set forth in the Reign of Queen Elizabeth. Edited by William Keatinge Clay. The Parker Society. Cambridge, 1847.

Masefield, John. *William Shakespeare.* Home University Library. London, 1911.

Measure for Measure. Edited by N. W. Bawcutt. The Oxford Shakespeare. Oxford: Clarendon Press, 1991.

Measure for Measure: A New Variorum Edition. Edited by Mark Eccles. Modern Language Association of America, 1980.

Measure for Measure. Edited by A. Quiller-Couch and J. Dover Wilson. The New Cambridge Shakespeare. Cambridge: University of Cambridge Press, 1922.

Miles, Rosalind. *The Problem of "Measure for Measure": A Historical Investigation.* London: Vision, 1976.

Muir, Kenneth. "The Duke's Soliloquies in *Measure for Measure.*" *Notes and Queries* 211 (1966): 135–36.

Nuttall, A. D. "Quid Pro Quo." *Shakespeare Studies* 4 (1951): 231–51.

Ornstein, Robert. *The Moral Vision of Jacobean Tragedy.* Madison: University of Wisconsin Press, 1960.

Powell, Jocelyn. "Theatrical *Tromp l'oeil* in *Measure for Measure.*" In *Shakespearian Comedy.* Stratford-upon-Avon Studies 14 (1972): 181-209.

Raleigh, Walter. *Shakespeare.* English Men of Letters. New York: Macmillan, 1907.

The Riverside Shakespeare. Edited by G. Blakemore Evans, et al. Boston: Houghton Mifflin, 1974.

Rosenberg, Marvin. "Shakespeare's Fantastic Trick: *Measure for Measure.*" *Studies in the Renaissance* 80 (1972): 51–72.

Ross, Lawrence J., ed. *Othello.* The Bobbs Merrill Shakespeare. Indianapolis, IN: Bobbs Merrill, 1974.

———. "Shakespeare's 'Dull Clown' and Symbolic Music." *Shakespeare Quarterly* 17 (1966): 107–28.

———. "Symbol and Structure in the *Secunda Pastorum*." *Comparative Drama* 1 (1967–68): 122–43. Reprinted in *Medieval English Drama: Essays Critical and Contextual*. Edited by Jerome Taylor and Alan H. Nelson. Chicago: University of Chicago Press, 1972.

Rossiter, A. P. *Angel with Horns: Fifteen Lectures on Shakespeare.* Edited by Graham Storey. London: Longmans, 1961.

Sandys, Edwin. *Sermons.* Edited by Joseph Ayre. The Parker Society. Cambridge, 1841.

Schanzer, Ernest. "The Marriage-Contracts in *Measure for Measure*." *Shakespeare Survey* 13 (1960): 81–89.

———. *The Problem Plays of Shakespeare: A Study of "Julius Caesar," "Measure for Measure," "Antony and Cleopatra."* New York: Schocken, 1963.

Shakespeare, William. *The First Folio of Shakespeare.* The Norton Facsimile. Prepared by Charlton Hinman. New York: Norton, 1968.

Shedd, Robert A. "The *Measure for Measure* of Shakespeare's 1604 Audience." Ph.D. diss., University of Michigan, 1953.

Skura, Meredith. "New Interpretations for Interpretations." *Boundary* 2 (1979): 39–59.

Smith, Henry. *The Magistrates Scripture.* In *Sermons.* London, 1591.

Sternfeld, Frederick. *Music in Shakespearean Tragedy.* Rev. ed. London and New York: Kegan Paul and Dover Press, 1967.

———. "*Troilus and Cressida*: Music for the Play." *English Institute Essays 1952.* Edited by Alan S. Downer. New York: Columbia University Press, 1954, 107–37.

Stevenson, David Lloyd. *The Achievement of Shakespeare's "Measure for Measure."* Ithaca: Cornell University Press, 1966.

———. "The Role of James I in Shakespeare's *Measure for Measure*." *ELH* 26 (1959): 188–208.

Stuart Royal Proclamations: vol. 1: *Royal Proclamations of King James I 1603–1625.* Edited by James F. Larkin and Paul L. Hughes. Oxford: Clarendon Press, 1973.

Swann, Charles. "Lucio: benefactor or malefactor." *Critical Quarterly* 29 (1987): 55–70.

Synodalia. Edited by Edward Cardwell. 2 vols. Oxford, 1842.

Taylor, Gary. "*Measure for Measure,* IV.ii.41–46." *Shakespeare Quarterly* 29 (1978): 419–21.

Taylor, Gary, and John Jowett. *Shakespeare Reshaped.* Oxford: Clarendon Press, 1993.

Tillyard, E. M. W. *Shakespeare's Problem Plays.* London: Chatto and Windus, 1950.

Tourneur, Cyril. *The Revenger's Tragedy.* Edited by Lawrence J. Ross. Regents Renaissance Drama. Lincoln: University of Nebraska Press, 1966.

Walker, Alice. "The Text of *Measure for Measure*." *The Review of English Studies* 34 (1983): 1–20.

Weil, Herbert Jr. "Form and Contexts in *Measure for Measure*." *Critical Quarterly* 12 (1970): 55–72.

————. Review of *The Achievement of "Measure for Measure,"* by D. L. Stevenson. *Shakespeare Studies* 3 (1967): 320–26.

————. "The Options of the Audience: Theory and Practice in Peter Brook's *Measure for Measure.*" *Shakespeare Survey* 25 (1972): 27–35.

Whetstone, George. *The Historie of Promos and Cassandra.* London, 1578.

Wilson, H. D. *King James VI and I.* London: Jonathan Cape, 1956.

Woods, D. T. B. "Tapestries of *The Seven Deadly Sins.*" *Burlington Magazine* 20 (1912): 210–22, 277–89.

Index